Silence in Heaven

SILENCE IN HEAVEN

A Book of Women's Preaching

Co-edited by
Susan Durber and Heather Walton

SCM PRESS LTD

0 334 01543 X

The quotations from Hildegard of Bingen on pages 135
and 137 are reprinted from *Meditations with Hildegard
of Bingen*, edited by Gabriele Uhlein, Copyright 1993,
Bear & Co. Inc., P.O. Box 2680, Santa Fe, NM 87504.

First published 1994
by SCM Press Ltd
26–30 Tottenham Road, London N1 4BZ

Phototypeset by Regent Typesetting, London
Printed in Great Britain by
Biddles, Guildford and King's Lynn

For our mothers and our daughters

Contents

Acknowledgment

The production of this book has been the result of collaboration by a number of women and we are glad to acknowledge it as the work of many hands.

In this spirit we have seen our own task as co-editors to entail the development of working methods that enabled us both to write and edit together. We have found this a challenging and enjoyable process and are proud that *Silence in Heaven* is a joint work, reflecting ideas and insights we have forged in partnership. That Heather Walton's name appears first on the cover is the result of an arbitrary decision and does not indicate any primacy of her work on the text.

We are most grateful to Rhoda Smith and Eve Kemp for all the work they have done in preparing the manuscript for publication.

Introduction

A Different Word

It is very exciting to see a volume of British women's sermons in print for the first time. Although women have been preaching from pulpit, platform and soapbox in this land for centuries, never before have words been set down for study and reflection. Nevertheless, there are still those who ask: 'Why publish a collection of sermons by women?'

The response that sermons by men have long been available in print whilst women's have not, have never been, would be reason enough to consider such a project. However, there are many more positive reasons to justify this undertaking. Some of these are related to the nature of preaching itself. In a culture where information has become a highly processed and packaged commodity the pulpit offers an increasingly rare platform for the consideration of issues which are seldom raised in other public forums. Opportunity exists for experimentation and innovation – albeit within defined if unarticulated boundaries. It is possible to see glimpses of new theological understandings emerging from within the life of a faith community and to discern the first stirrings of changes taking place as preachers grapple to name God in response to the circumstances of their day.

Naturally, all these factors apply equally to the preaching of men and women. But the fact that the 'word of God' has been heard for centuries from the mouths of men means that many women are especially conscious of both the difficulties and opportunities that fall to them as preachers and have begun to reflect upon them. This reflective activity is born of an awareness that to be a woman preacher is to be 'different'. The woman who preaches can assume much less about her own position and the tradition in which she stands than her male colleagues. As many of us have been made acutely aware, merely to speak from the body of a woman is to present a challenge to some congregations. An entirely conventional sermon may take on new resonances as it is delivered by a person whose body presents an unconventional icon of authority.

We have found that even those who are entirely supportive of women preachers may discover themselves responding differently to a message of love and power told to them from a woman's lips. This is because the ways of understanding what loving and strength may be are differentially associated with women and men in our society – hence the fury over the debate about whether God loves us as a mother or a father loves. Such is the force of the cultural associations that surround us that it is arguable that a woman in the pulpit always presents a different perspective even if her sermon appears to be indistinguishable in its content from that of her male counterparts. To be a woman is to carry with you numerous symbolic associations in a society which is fundamentally divided along gender lines.

In the past women preachers have found it necessary to struggle against the many assumptions that are made about us and to stress our common calling alongside men. Anything which might distinguish our contribution as particularly feminine has been regarded as potentially distracting or likely to call our vocation into question and thus carefully edited out. However, we are now coming to realize that our difference from men may not only constrain us but might also be a source of radical potential. We can use the alternative understandings we have forged from our experience of marginality in a male defined culture and church to challenge that culture at its heart.

A Word in Time

When a sense of the disturbing power of women's difference is coupled with an awareness of the possibilities that the pulpit offers to present new ideas exciting things can happen. Although seldom formally articulated there is a growing sense amongst women preachers that the conventions which surround the activity of preaching must not be allowed to restrain our creativity. The exploration of new forms of proclamation which was nurtured initially in supportive feminist groups is now informing our practice at the heart of church life. We have learnt to celebrate our role as interpreters and shapers of tradition and take pride in the fact that women are leading the way in discovering how the activity of preaching might develop in the future.

This collection, therefore, appears at a significant moment in the development of women's preaching and the contributions have been chosen with this fact in mind. We hope both to reflect and reinforce the movement taking place. For this reason we have not attempted to bring together a representative sample of sermons but have rather selected on the basis of some key principles.

1. Women should be visible in the text. Whilst this sounds like a very modest requirement it should be considered alongside the fact that the majority of sermons preached make no reference to women at all. God is usually described in male imagery, biblical references are frequently male-centred and illustrations most commonly drawn from the lives of 'great men' of faith.

2. Just as women are often invisible in what is preached so the issues that specifically relate to women are not given voice. There is a profound silence from our pulpits on vital subjects like rape, abuse and violence against women. Whilst it is terrible that these issues should not be raised it is equally appalling that the joy women experience, for example in sexuality and procreation, likewise remains unmentioned and therefore uncelebrated as a vehicle of revelation.

Many of the sermons in this book break the silence that surrounds women's experience with the dual intention of helping us to understand ourselves better and also gaze upon a different face of God. For when we begin to name what has previously been unnamed in Christian thinking new metaphors and symbols are forged that can function most powerfully as a stimulus to faith. Whilst making apparent what has formally been unregarded is a valuable contribution in itself, the effects of so doing go far beyond righting a current existing imbalance in favour of men.

3. Women have also developed new ways of reading the Bible by drawing on feminist theory and insights. They have become

suspicious of the traditional distinctions between exegesis and eisegesis and have affirmed the difference it makes to read from a different place. Many of the sermons in this book view old texts in new ways, recognizing the construction of the texts within patriarchal culture and also seizing the power of an interpreter to resist the text or to read it against the grain. Feminist hermeneutics has made a difference to preaching.

4. As women struggle to express themselves they have found that the existing forms of communication and the traditional concepts are inadequate for their needs. How to preach and what to preach are not questions that can be answered by simply studying past and present practices, something quite new and different is being sought. A number of the contributions made here are courageous experiments in very different ways of constructing a sermon. They contain the potential for renewing both the practice of preaching and the doing of theology.

A Word in Crisis

The sermons in *Silence in Heaven* find their place within a response to a kind of 'crisis' for preaching – and indeed theology. Particularly since the 1960s there have been many voices expressing unease with the traditional model of preaching. The pulpit has provided a place of extraordinary power within many congregations and preachers have used that power, often with great effect. But in a church whose people are increasingly wary of clerical dominance and authoritarian modes of teaching, the pulpit has looked increasingly shaky. Why should one person (and usually a male person) occupy this space week after week? Cannot the word of God be heard more effectively in a discussion or reflection group where all may find a voice? Isn't the passivity normally expected of a congregation listening to a sermon a denial of the gifts God has given them and an implied rejection of the 'priesthood of all believers'? Why should one voice be the bearer of truth? John Fiske, in his book *Reading the Popular*, describes religion in decisively authoritarian terms.

> ... the religious congregation is powerless, led like sheep through the rituals and means, forced to 'buy' the truth on

offer, all the truth, not selective bits of it. Where the interests of the Authority on High differ from those of the Congregation down Low, the congregation has no power to negotiate: all accommodations are made by the powerless, subjugated to the great truth. (Fiske, 1989; pp. 13–14)

As the church has taken seriously the critique of its life which is reflected in Fiske's harsh words, so it has struggled with the genre of preaching and asked searching questions about its future. There have also been less sophisticated but equally telling criticisms of preaching; where else do we sit mute before a speaker raised so high above contradiction – isn't preaching an outmoded form of communication designed for days before radio and television? The 'decline' of preaching can be seen clearly in developments in church architecture. Now, even churches where preaching has traditionally provided the climax of worship are being redesigned to express the increasing importance of sacraments and symbols and of the 'fellowship' of the people with one another.

Certainly in Britain the response of many women to this crisis has been to abandon preaching altogether. While women may occupy the powerful space of the preacher when invited into traditional churches, it has often been the case that when in a space they can call their own, women have not engaged in preaching at all. It is significant that in the introduction to the worship material in the book *Women Included*, no mention of preaching is made. Though it is clear that whilst some of the women of the community are themselves preachers in other places, the practice when the community worships is to follow the reading or readings with a group reflection. Emphasis is placed on framing new liturgies which will be creative, participative and engaging all the senses, but preaching, it seems, is laid aside. While recognizing the very serious critique under which traditional models of preaching stand, the sermons in this book are offered as part of a struggle to name new paradigms for preaching – not to revive a dying form, but to offer new ways in which a single voice from a woman's body may be a source of wisdom and gospel for the church. An alternative strategy to the abandonment of preaching is to search for new paradigms which will seek to break the authoritarian and closed structure of old models and which will encourage the naming of faith in more open and liberating ways.

Many of the sermons in the book echo new styles of preaching which have also been affirmed by men; the use of imagination, the self-conscious taking account of context and the telling of stories. However, it is significant that these ways of speaking which men have found 'new' have always been characteristic of women's discourse. They are also ways which, in themselves, in their very method, style and form, subvert the authoritarian model of preaching. In engaging the 'hearer' in imaginative listening, the preacher gives over power to the congregation. The imagination, when unloosed, brings freedom. In taking seriously context and contextualization, the preacher admits openly that the words spoken are not 'eternal truth', but situated knowledge, knowledge for someone. In telling stories, the preacher offers a 'text' which is open and plural and which gives the 'reader/hearer' a task to do of interpretation. Women preachers, in these suggested new paradigms, will make full use of such methods and styles because they embody a form of speaking which struggles not to be authoritarian or prescriptive, but open and inviting. This in itself is not unique to women, but it is significant that these ways of speaking have been long established as part of women's story. As those who have been the victims of male authority and men's absolute truths, women are likely to speak with a new voice.

There are other ways too in which new paradigms for preaching drawn from the insights, experience and 'marginality' of women may lead to new hope. As the sermons in this book testify, women are likely to speak more directly from the personal, to name experience in the pulpit which we have previously been told not to name. Here again is the commitment to a mode of knowledge which does not claim to have access to 'absolute truth', but which recognizes and celebrates its own relatedness to a particular life or community. As women speak from their position from outside the mainstream of our culture, they will shake the apparently solid foundations of what we had previously held to be authoritative. So, women's response to the 'crisis' of peaching may be not, after all, to abandon it, but to speak with new voices and from a different place. Women will speak not from the high and lofty pulpit, above contradiction and dispute, but from their own place in the church and world with openness and provisionality, with wit and wisdom.

There will be those who will accuse us of compromise and pragmatism, of collaborating with the oppressors by venturing into their space. They will warn us of the dangers of such strategies and accuse us of wanting power for ourselves on terms which we should despise. However, there is more than one way to overcome an enemy. In this case, subversion and revisioning may be as valid as retreat, though many women will enter the pulpit with fear and trembling. It would be true to say that the sermons in the book represent a variety of strategies within a commitment to a renewal of preaching and a claiming of preaching as some-thing women can and should do in ways which are radically different from men. Most have been peached within the context of a local church and some by the woman who serves the church as its minister. Some have been preached on 'special' occasions – women's gatherings or events. Others have never been preached because what they say cannot yet be said in the churches. These very different voices, speaking from different places and in different tones, struggle to break the silence.

Words of God

The 'crisis' which has produced a radical rethinking of the art of preaching can be seen as symptomatic of a deeper shift taking place well beyond the confines of the church.

We live in an age where all confident, self-authenticating claims to knowledge have come under scrutiny. Systems that purposed to explain the nature of human existence, or to offer blueprints for a better future, now appear frighteningly flawed. We have become acutely aware of the dangers inherent in 'grand narratives' which seem simply to describe the way things are but in fact themselves create rigid rules; setting limits to our expecta-tions and reinforcing power relationships that exist in society.

A result of this changed understanding is that what has formerly regarded as self evidently good and true is now treated with suspicion. We have learnt to ask what alternative perspec-tives, representing the wisdom of those outside the mainstream, have been silenced in order that one voice can speak with authority.

Feminism has been a significant force in developing the critical spirit of our times. It has played both a destructive and creative role. It has been destructive in that it has sought to expose the way our culture is built not upon eternal truths but rather ideologies which mirror the interests and experience of men. However, once the authority ceded to a notion of truth that stands outside us and over against us is challenged, space is opened up to develop new and creative ways of knowing. As we have seen, the insights of art, story, vision and imagination are re-valued when it is recognized that there is no bright, shining truth against which the shafts of illumination they generate can be compared. Similarly, because it is recognized that knowledge is always partial and always produced out of particular contexts women have become more confident in declaring our own insights valid. We have learnt to value the truths we forge from our own experience and declare such 'situated knowledge' a starting point for interpreting the world that is just as significant as any other.

These insights have been very important to feminists engaged in theology as it is immediately evident how often what was taken for the voice of God has in reality been the voice of men. We have approached our own tradition both as destroyers and creators determined to show how women's insights have been excluded from our faith story and to find new ways in which that story can be told.

This way of approaching theology has far reaching implications best illustrated in preaching. It challenges 'logocentrism', understanding based on sure and single truths, with a conviction that God speaks in many different forms and in many different voices. What has been repressed is brought forward to confront what was formally exalted; body speaks to spirit, darkness to light, mystery to certainty and story to the library of systematic theology.

These Words

The sermon, a piece of theological work performed within a particular community and manifestly coming from a particular voice, may embody well new and creative models of knowing. Preaching is not the place where the eternal truths are made accessible, but the place in which theology may be formed. As the occasion when the theology of particular peoples and communities comes into being, preaching can be the source of theology. Preaching informs theology. So, these sermons have been collected together, not to illustrate how new theological insights are being conveyed to people in churches (or how they might be conveyed), but rather to show how preaching is a site of struggle and a crucible of theological fire. The 'pulpit' is a workplace for theologians and women are doing theology there.

In gathering these sermons together, we have sought to present new paradigms for preaching and theology. This volume brings together work by Christian and post-Christian women, by heterosexual women and lesbian women, by women who live at the centre of the church's life and by those who live at its margins. There are many different voices to be heard. There are also others that should be heard. It is a real weakness of the book that no sermons by black women are included.

We have called the book *Silence in Heaven* – a title we chose for its resonance and ambiguity as much as for any one of its potential meanings. It could express grief over the silence of women which is only now beginning to be broken. It could call for silence in the court of heaven so that women's voices may be heard. It could describe the stony silence with which heaven responds to the wisdom of women or perhaps the reverence with which the angels hear the long forgotten music of female voices. Who can say? We hope that as the silence is broken by the words in this book and by other words shared in many churches and groups, so something new will come to birth.

Speaking from the Body

Contemporary women preachers who seek to use their bodily experience as a resource when proclaiming their faith struggle against centuries of tradition. Indeed, one of the most serious accusations that can be levelled against the Christian faith must surely be its responsibility over two millennia for many crimes against women's bodies.

Born of two cultural parents, the Hellenistic and Jewish traditions of the ancient world, early Christianity inherited many negative ideas about women which the young church embraced rather than challenged. From Greek thought came the identification of women with the despised world of flesh, matter and corruption – in contrast to the male realm of spirit and reason. The Judaism of the time had itself absorbed some of these ideas and contributed its own taboos against women drawing close to the sacred during times when their bodies were held to be particularly dangerous and potentially polluting, e.g. during menstruation and after childbirth.

Although Jewish regulations concerning 'purity' must not be confused with Christian thinking about 'sinfulness', the idea that there is something about the body of a woman which makes problematic her relation to the spiritual God has been profoundly influential and goes back to our deepest roots. The misogynist views of many 'church fathers' are notorious and their comments about women sit unhappily with their lofty pronouncements on the faith. All this has been well documented in the work of women like Rosemary Ruether and Karen Armstrong and there is not space to dwell in detail upon it here. Tertullian's (in)famous comments represent such thinking in its plainest form. For this holy man the flesh of woman was the route through which evil

entered creation and he urged faithful Christian women to keep
this knowledge ever before them.

> And do you not know that you are each an Eve? The sentence
> of God on this sex of yours lives in this age: the guilt must of
> necessity live too. You are the devil's gateway.

Given undoubtedly negative official attitudes to women's
physicality and sexuality it is easy to understand how many
profoundly damaging developments took place within cultures
where Christianity became dominant. Feminists have justly
called the church to account for the holocaust of women during
the mediaeval 'witch hunts' and for the sacralization of virginity
and motherhood which have regulated women's sexuality to the
present day. However, alongside this dark history, another tradition has always existed and women preachers who 'speak from
their bodies' today are inheritors of this legacy.

Elaine Pagels has shown how some Gnostic groups within early
Christianity confidently asserted the appropriateness of the
female form as a vehicle of divine revelation. Although the visions
and prophecies of Gnostics, and the later similar ideas of
Montanists and Shakers, were quickly pronounced heretical,
corresponding traditions lived on in the heart of the church
through the mystical tradition. The English mystic Julian of
Norwich speaks plainly and movingly of the comfort and
sustenance of Christ her mother and even male spiritual writers
make use, although sparingly, of metaphors drawn from
women's fertile and nurturing bodies to speak of a God who
cannot be contained by conventional religious formulas.

Nevertheless, despite the existence of this precious counter
tradition, it is understandable that women preachers admitted to
the pulpit since the birth of non-conformity have been reticent
about speaking explicitly from the hidden life of their bodies. In
this they have shared a suspicion with their sisters in other public
and professional spheres that to do so would result in their
ghettoization and confinement to a specific 'female' sphere. Often
they have rather chosen to stress a common rationality, a univer-
sal human nature and an unembodied spirituality.

This might be regarded as a prudent strategy given the
suspicion and hostility that many women preachers have

experienced. However, it could be argued that the apparently neutral speaking position women have sought to occupy has in fact been one in which the metaphors and symbols they use are largely drawn from male experience. Furthermore, women speaking in conventional terms of a God who is father, a saviour who is brother and disciples who are men of God are encouraging the women who hear them to assume the position of male subjects in their spiritual imaginings and unwittingly to obscure their lived (and bodily) experience as women of faith.

Many Christian women have been stimulated to think more about such issues because of the challenges of the women's movement. Germaine Greer asserted in the heady early days of feminism that women had no idea how much their physicality was hated and feared in Western culture. Violent and porno-graphic images are the extreme symptom of such hatred; the common imagery of art and advertising being the day to day manifestations of women's bodies used as objects for exploita-tion and pleasure. It is hard now to imagine how revolutionary her call for women to touch and explore their own bodies and to speak plainly of their pleasure and their pain then appeared.

In more recent years much debate has taken place within feminism as to how fundamental having the body of a woman is to the approach we take to life. Some would assert that women are essentially constituted as respecters of life and growth by their ability to bear children. Others would see social forces as much more influential in shaping female identity. While this debate has raged there has been a growing consensus that the world of language and culture has been largely silent about insights drawn from women's bodily experience. The shock and distaste that many experience when such subjects are raised in church is evidence to support this view. Christian feminists have sought to break such taboos, relating the insights they have gained from their physical experiences to their faith in God.

Very naturally it was to maternal imagery that women first turned in their attempts to speak holy words from their bodies. A rich new resource for preaching and praying was generated from the celebration of conception, birth and nurture. How-ever, having the body of a woman is not simply a positive and wholesome experience as anyone who has experienced pregnancy and labour might testify. The realities of infertility, illness, rape and abuse are also bodily experiences through which women need to be able to interpret the divine. Women aware of the inseparable joys and sorrows of the flesh are claiming both life and death as vehicles of revelation. These developments take the issue of speaking from the body a great deal further than the formative arguments surrounding the appropriateness of naming God as mother. Nevertheless, there is a long road still to travel.

Sexuality and suffering are still rarely named within a Christian tradition that prefers to speak of the spirit rather than the body, light rather than darkness and a God who creates life but bears no responsibility for pain and dying. Women who have begun to preach from their bodies are not merely redressing an existing imbalance and enriching the storehouse of Christian metaphors and symbols but are also provoking new theological debates close to the very heart of the faith.

STANDING IN THE STABLE

Luke 2.1–20

'How silently, how silently, the wondrous gift is given.' Or so the carol goes.

But come with me for a moment. In your imagination, come with me. Let me take you to the stable. It is a dark, dark night, and we can hardly see to make our way down the track behind the houses. It is cold too. In some ways, we would rather be sitting around a bright fireside, talking with friends into the corners of the night, watching the firelight reflected in our smiles. Yet we have come tonight for a special reason. We have come to see the new baby. So we do not mind the darkness too much. And with our excitement, we do not allow the cold to penetrate too deeply.

We push the stable door. Inside it is not much warmer. But it is just as dark. If anything, it is even darker. Pitch dark, as dark as water at the bottom of a well. And we can see nothing at all – not even our hand in front of our face. We stand, motionless, in the hopes that our eyes will become accustomed to the darkness, and that soon we shall at least begin to make out the shadows. But the darkness is deep, and we can see nothing.

But listen! 'I'll never manage this! I'll just never manage this!' A scream, a shout of pain. And then quiet. Then another scream, and quiet again. We huddle closer to each other in the darkness, as if to protect ourselves from the realization that we have come too soon. Too soon. The birth is not complete. We take each other by the hand, and stand without a word, stunned by the inappropriateness of arriving before time.

Another shout, as if it is dredged from the deepest pain. And then quiet. Shall we go out again, discreetly, and pretend that we were never here? But now that we have come, we cannot prise ourselves away. The pain holds us. We have become part of the relentless rhythm of silence and screaming, and we cannot prise ourselves away.

'I'm never going through this again! I can't! I can't!' There is another scream, this time louder, tearing into us, and forcing us to be part of the pain. How much longer must we wait in the darkness? How much longer must we share the agony of this woman? How much longer before the coming of this baby?

'How silently, how silently, the wondrous gift is given.' Or so the carol goes ... But do you still believe it, now that you are standing in the stable?

'The little Lord Jesus no crying he makes.'
Or so the carol goes.

The baby has still not come. How long have we been here? We cannot think how long. Time has been strangely suspended. Each moment has been a time on its own. We have been held in the present, drawn into the pain of this woman for whom nothing else exists, not even the darkness. How long can we have been here? Surely dawn will soon be breaking.

This is no place to have a baby. Just feel how it is in here. The baby will be born into cold and darkness. And there is no water. No water to wash the baby. Can it be true that there is nowhere else for this woman to go? With all the buildings that there are in this town, there must be a room somewhere for her. Someone must be willing to take her in. Are the doors of this town always so unwelcoming to the stranger? Are they always shut to the one who brings life?

The screams have been getting more rapid. There has been a breathlessness to take our own breath away, and we have been accelerated into a rhythm of cries and calm that has confused us, and left us holding to each other, as if to ease the trial of suspense. Then suddenly, there is a cry to break into us, a scream to break the rhythm and to hang, haunting the darkness. Then quiet. This time a deep quiet. A quiet of relief and exhaustion. We wait, silently, sharing the quiet, not daring to punctuate it even by our breathing ... And then the sound we have been waiting for ... Listen ... A new voice cuts the darkness. The baby is crying. The baby is crying his new life to us!

'The little Lord Jesus no crying he makes.' Or so the carol goes ... But do you still believe it, now that you are standing in the stable?

But now that we are standing here, we begin to understand something about ourselves. In our believing, in our living, we have been like the Christmas carols. We have preferred to say that all is silent. We have wanted to be deaf to the realities which surround us. We have wanted a world where children's crying is never heard, and women's screams are blotted out. We have wanted a world in which virtuous women are the ones who hold their peace, and in which virtuous children are the ones whose voices never reach our ears.

But now that we are standing in the stable, we are beginning to understand. Every Christmas we have come back, hymn book in hand, eager to have our ears blocked once again under the magnetic glow of the candles. Every year we have come back to sing of the ideal woman, of the 'mother mild', and of 'her maiden bliss'. Every year we have come back to hear how nobody at Bethlehem was willing to offer shelter to a pregnant woman going into labour, and how she had to give birth in a sordid cowshed. And every year we have come back to sing that this was surely a 'blessed morn' and that Mary, the picture of virtue, the 'virgin pure', 'the lowly maiden' was nothing but contentment. The mother 'did nothing take in scorn', we have come back to sing.

And every year we have returned to hear the old story: how the meek maiden aquiesces to the will of the angel. We have come to renew our old picture of the virtuous woman: ready aquiescence, ready agreement, ready servanthood, no questions asked. And then, as we have heard the story of the shepherds' lifting their voices in joyful praise, we have listened again, intently, to the portrait of the perfect woman – the perfect woman who treasures these things in her heart and in the face of all her hardship, never says a word.

And it has been the same with the children. Every year we have come to sing of the perfect child: the child who never cries, who lays his sweet head down, and who, once 'in slumber reclining' is worthy of the worship of angels. Every year we have come to renew our picture of the child who is mild, obedient and good, the child who is always so silent, that 'no ear may hear his coming'. Yes, it is true, we understand now. We have wanted our cocooned cotton-wool deafness. We have wanted women whose pain need never come to our ears and children whose crying need not be heard.

The dawn is beginning to break. There is quiet in the stable, and the light is beginning, just beginning to penetrate. The mother is there, in the corner, in the shadows. We can only barely make her out. There is joy in the way she puts her child to her breast. But she is exhausted. She has discovered a tiredness she never knew before. Look at the way she holds herself. Her body is drooping, immobile, as if she could not draw another movement from out of herself. All the pain, all the struggle, all the toil, shows in her demeanour, the wornness of her expression.

So now that the shadows are lifting in the stable, we understand something else. Always we used to think that God could be born into our world easily. We used to think that God's new life would come to our troubled world just by saying the word, just by offering our 'meek souls' to receive him. We used to believe that faith demanded no effort. But now we realize that we were wrong. Now we have stood in the stable. Now we know that there is no birth without pain, no new life without struggle, no joy without fatigue. Now we know that God cannot be born into our world of conflict and famine and grief unless there is struggle.

Yes, we are standing in the stable and we are beginning to understand. God does not belong to some false world which pretends that there is no pain. God does not belong to a tinsel stable with full sanitation and cosy romantic lighting, or to some fairy-tale land where people find life comfortable and where homelessness is sweet. No. God belongs to our world, our world of pain and darkness, which yearns for the joy and the new life which only struggle and anguish and patience will bring. Now we are beginning to understand. God is to be found not in never-never Christmas card dreams, but deep, deep in the relentless rhythm of screams and silence, of joy and pain. It is there that God draws time and eternity together.

The dawn is nearly here. In the half-light, we turn to each other. Tell me, why were you willing to come with me to the stable? Think, and tell me from your heart. Was it because you wanted to feel Christmassy? I expect it may have been. Or was it because the Christmas story is a beautiful story, and you wanted to hear it again? That too would be a good reason. Or was it because you wanted to remember past Christmasses and all the people who have been dear to you? Yes, perhaps you came with me because you wanted to remember.

But perhaps also you came with me because you thought that God could only be found in some kind of comfortable fairy-tale world. Perhaps it was because you thought that you could not find God in your world, in your darkness, or in your struggle. Perhaps it was because you thought you could not find God in your own life, with all its relentless rhythm of calm and crying.

Do you still believe it, now that you are standing in the stable?

Mary Cotes

THE FACE OF CHRIST

II Corinthians 4 (AV)

From the reading of II Corinthians chapter 4, keep a few words and phrases especially in mind:

Christ as the image of God
the face of Christ
light   knowledge   grace   glory

and in particular, verse 6:

For it is the God who said, 'Let light shine out of darkness', who has shone in our heart to give the light of the knowledge of the glory of God in the face of Jesus Christ.

Here then is an apostle, by God's *mercy* called to a ministry of proclamation, saved by the mercy he now proclaims, turned from persecuting others who had proclaimed the gospel before him. He reminds us, as he puts it, that the life of Jesus was not simply manifested in our flesh in the past – the glory of God seen in the face of one dying then dead but raised by God, and still to be manifested in our flesh. How do we get some sort of sense of God's continued gracious self-giving to us? – think of Christ's face, he suggests. Recognizing God is somewhat indirect-God is not available to us to grab and snatch at and keep for ourselves, or dish out like doses of medicine brought out from under our locks and keys. But God's initiative and grace is there for us if we know where to focus our attention – on a face, a particular face.

And this comes from someone acutely sensitive to idolatry, the idolatry of things, of persons, or words – anything that will block off God, or hinder or confuse us in our efforts to respond to God's grace, God's generosity – a grace and a generosity that yet has a face. So keep in mind the question. Does this metaphor of Christ's face provide us with the sort of focus we need without tipping us unawares into something like idolatry? Think of how attractive that legend of the *true icon* has been – the longing expressed in the story of Veronica, the woman who blots the sweaty bleeding face of Christ on his way to execution, so that we can say, 'Here it is, shall *we* let *you* see him?' Any 'ikons' we have are meant to be *transparent* to what lies beyond them, not to be objects we fix on.

And if the face of Christ is to be a face we can each of us in our inexhaustible differences all focus on, it's crucial that we shouldn't have too fixed an image of Christ in our imaginations. For think of human faces – fourteen different bones, I believe, and at least one hundred different muscles just beneath the skin, criss-crossing in extraordinary ways, capable of an astonishing variety of subtle, complex and beautiful movements – some not so beautiful too. The skin is more or less lustrous and transparent, coloured in different ways, and to different depths, as are our eyes and hair.

We spend a lot of time on our faces – think of what human beings hang in their ears or pin into their noses or even their lips. We decorate our skin with cosmetics (not just for the stage) and we scar it into patterns or use tattoos. We sometimes wear patches. We take trouble to frame our faces by the way we shape our hair or wear wigs or – some of us – grow moustaches or beards. We wear hats and necklaces, sometimes masks or veils. We wear scent behind our ears and aftershave on our skins.

Some of the faces which intrigue us the most are those of people who have great insight into others, whilst themselves having faces which can be enigmatic, ambiguous, capable of subtle change, as with some great actors. And faces can terrify us – if deliberately obscured to menace us – wearing a stocking mask, or kept in shadow whilst we are mercilessly placed in a blazing light. By contrast, the faces we most want to see are those who share the light with us – light we can bear – those we love and trust and long for, as they love and trust and long for us. Imagine the ways in which we look for one another at railway stations or at bus depots or any other sort of meeting place.

To return to Christ's face from ours – Christ's face can't be meant to menace us. This isn't God in a stocking mask, but is more likely to be akin to those who have the intriguing or enigmatic or ambiguous qualities of some great actor – someone who may have great insight into others, but who like our friends wants to share the light with us, wants to be seen, wants to communicate, to give, to show us what we are, what we might be capable of, what we might be capable of becoming. And if it's a face that somehow enables us to glimpse God, it will be a face which will help us to recognize what we're *really* like, not just what we think we're like, help us to face it, to face up to it, as we say, and yet not be crippled by what we see. Paul, you remember, by God's *mercy* had been called from persecution to proclamation, and somewhere in the experience of this mercy must have been moments of appalled recognition at what he was, what he'd been doing.

And if we were to glance back at an earlier passage, chapter 2 verse 10, we'll find him saying, 'for if I forgave anything, to whom I forgave it, for your sakes forgave I it, in the person of Christ, lest Satan should get an advantage of us.' Since we've got into something of a muddle recently over this phrase 'in the person of Christ', translators offer another interpretation or translation of the words, 'as the the representative of Christ', which may help a bit. The point is that Paul does not suppose he's a kind of literal or physical stand-in for Christ. It's rather that what he does in God's mercy is done in the presence of Christ and under his judgment. But we still need to ask, how do *we* find the face of Christ? I pointed out that the faces we most want to see will be those we love and trust and long for as they love and trust and long for us. These will be the faces of people quite capable of telling us when we've made idiots of ourselves or have hurt or harmed someone or something but who will go on loving and trusting and longing for us – here is something of the life of Jesus manifest in our bodies.

Let me briefly give you one example, to provoke you to think of your own – drawn not from our present century, but from the late thirteenth and early fourteenth, from Dante's life and Dante's *Divine Comedy*. Dante wrote what Dorothy Sayers called a drama of the soul's choice – a drama played out so that we in our turn might learn the taste of heaven, hear of the possibility of ecstasy, joy, and 'the love that moves the sun and the other stars'. In the very last part of the *Divine Comedy* and I've just quoted the last line, 'The love that moves the sun and the other stars', Dante tries to write of the Trinity in non-human-face terms, as three spheres of light.

> The first mirrored the next, as though it were
> Rainbow from Rainbow, and the third seemed flame
> Breathes equally from each of the first pair.

Yet one of these spheres he wrote

> Seemed in itself, and in its own self-hue,
> Limned with our image; for which cause mine eyes
> were altogether drawn and held thereto.

And whose image is *our* image? Dante, you may recall, had loved as a child someone he loved as a living woman, and whom he went on loving even after she died, and he became an adult man married to Gemma, with children of their own. As Charles Williams once wrote, the Beatrice of the *Comedy* is perhaps more like Gemma than even Dante quite knew. Of Beatrice he wrote: 'I say that when she appeared from any direction, then, in the hope of her wondrous salutation, there was no enemy left to me; rather there smote into me a flame of charity, which made me forgive every person who had ever injured me; and if at that moment anybody had put a question to me about anything whatsoever, my answer would have been simply "Love", with a countenance clothed in humility.'

Beatrice had become to him what he could in his turn be for someone else, or we in turn could be for one another – a grace-bearer, though it's a somewhat unnerving prospect! It's as though he takes the sort of thing Paul talks about – the life of Jesus manifest in our mortal flesh-entirely seriously, much more seriously than we do. And in the pageant of the sacrament in the *Divine Comedy* Dante has addressed to Beatrice words from the eucharistic liturgy: 'Benedictus qui venis' – Blessed art thou that comest (in the name of the Lord). Through seeing her after longing for her eyes and her smile, her sight of him in turn, and the words they exchange, giving and receiving from one another, Dante shows us the mutuality of love, grace, mercy and forgiveness, even the glory, of which Paul writes. Dante's words for prayer are 'I in-thee me as thou in meëst thee', whilst both of them remain very much themselves, and are able to help one another finally to enjoy God – those spheres of the Trinity, one of which is as Dante put it, 'Limned with our image'. Dante gives us an idea of what Paul talks about when he writes of 'the glory of God in the face of Jesus Christ' and the life of Jesus 'made manifest in our mortal flesh'. And turning it around, so to speak, I can find in this some encouragement to think that Paul might have been a bit more like Dante than we allow for, which is a cheering thought.

In any event, as I've suggested, it's as though we don't take Paul as seriously as maybe Dante did – and to our own hurt. We don't expect to see grace and glory on one another's faces as we meet in the street, and I don't see why we shouldn't. And if we don't, maybe our expectations of how to see one another aren't right, for if we can't enjoy one another, how do we expect to glimpse God's glory in Christ's face? And how can we expect relationships between women and men in the church ever to be what they could be until and unless we take the risks of paying attention to one another in the way Paul and Dante encourage – and so see God's glory in Christ's face reflected in one another – see it, praise it, and love it.

Ann Loades

INVISIBLE CHRISTIANS*

Mark 11.15–1

Being here tonight cannot be a painless experience. To speak openly about Christian survivors of sexual abuse is to make a call to a new ministry, one not yet developed in this country. Mary Pallauer says 'Ministry occurs when the skin of the soul is rubbed raw'. Many of us Christian survivors have had the skin of our souls rubbed raw; the result has been both anger and pain. For me the skin of my soul was rubbed raw when I was sexually abused by my brother in childhood, raped by an Anglican vicar when I was twenty-three years old, yet again, rubbed raw upon hearing about the lives of other Christian survivors and by experiencing the silence of the Christian church and community.

The silence about our presence has been amazing. In many places we as a church are so quiet about sexual abuse you might

---

* A sermon given at Great St Mary's Cambridge in October 1992.

think it is approved of! We survivors of sexual abuse pose such a challenge to traditional church teachings about the family, child-rearing, women, men, power and sexuality that the issue is avoided if at all possible.

With research showing that one in five women and one in twelve men are sexually abused in childhood how can the church truly believe it doesn't happen in good Christian families? This is a myth. Ninety-five per cent of abusers are men and despite the clear prohibition of incest in Leviticus 6–18 the majority of reported aggressors are regular church attenders. It is difficult to measure someone's 'Christianity' but researchers do report that these adult males tend to be very devout, moralistic and conservative in their religious beliefs.

In Australia the Anglican Diocese of Melbourne's research project (1989–90) on 'Sexual and Family Violence in Congregations' reports: 'Far from being a sanctuary for victims the Church has within established traditions, theology and practice systematic factors that serve to hide its perpetrators and victims of violence'. There is a belief that men have ownership of the members of the household, that the man is the head of the household and may do within the sanctity of his own home what he will with both the body of his wife and his children which he perceives as belonging to him – his property. These beliefs go back into antiquity and are enshrined in most of the dominant religious texts of the world.

Man is seen as the image of God (the only image). Man is therefore idealized, seen as God-like, never abusing children or women. For many men this God-like status seems to give them 'permission' to do as they wish (sanctioned by the church by the complicity of silence) which is not too difficult since women and children have conversely been indoctrinated to be submissive and to obey.

Incest is not only caused by the offender but also by the churches and society through structural denial of, and contempt for, women and children and their experiences.

The abuse of women and children is likely to continue until we are able to diminish the patriarchal assumptions that govern both the family and society.

Rev. Marie Fortune, a wonderful woman in this ministry asks

us to do several things. She says that churches need to tell the truth, to acknowledge the harm done to victims. She says in expressing this acknowledgment to the victims, belief and out-rage are fully communicated. Churches also need to break the silence. This involves the deprivatization of secrets. By dealing with the offence openly we break down the secrecy that has sustained the abuse for so long. The silence only protects the offenders from the consequences of their act. It does not protect the victim or future victims. Finally, we must hear the whole story for so many people tend to minimize the seriousness of sexual abuse. It is one way of dealing with the horror of its truth. De-minimizing – being willing to hear and believe the experiences of victims is a means of standing with them.

As well as considering the structural androcratic, patriarchal nature of our Christian communities which facilitate and encourage abuse in our families, Christian communities must begin to name and see this sexual violence to children. Once named, no longer invisible, sexual abuse will move from the margin of discussion to the centre of discussion.

We must have an intentional breaking of the silence. We must speak about the issues. Both clergy and laity have a responsibility to say the words; rape, incest, child sexual abuse, battering. We must not hide behind euphemisms. What we are talking about is children being penetrated, being raped orally, vaginally, anally. Children being kissed, fondled, touched in sexual ways which violate their bodies.

Some clergy and communities have been afraid to learn about these private terrors because of antiquated notions of family and marital bliss, inadequacy fears in terms of counselling abilities, close friendships. But a problem inadequately named cannot be adequately addressed. This is the environment in which adult Christian survivors live. What have been the effects for them of living in this androcratic patriarchal society and being abused?

As a survivor I do not have a healthy image of myself as a woman. God was always presented to me as male and good. Men were good and powerful, women were weak and sinful. These Christian messages I received growing up combined with the sexual violation of my little child female body served to convince me that I was indeed a truly bad and unworthy person. Since God and male were inextricably linked then I, as female, must be deserving of this. I was bad. This was confirmed for me several years ago by a Catholic priest who, upon hearing I had been sexually abused as a child, said to me 'Go to confession and confess your sins of impurity'. My last memory of being abused is at the age of fourteen, but I have other earlier memories as well, so it seems incredible that he was asking me to confess impurity at that age. He didn't say anything about my abuser. We are always blamed for our violation because we are seen as the sinful person (woman). We are also blamed for our suffering: 'If you are a good Christian God will treat you kindly or take care of you or make your prosper as a reward for your goodness. If you suffer it is a sign that you must not be a good Christian or God is displeased with you.' I have been told that because my suffering does not go away I must not be praying enough. I have heard of another survivor being told she is not being healed by God because she is doing something to block the healing!

I still perceive God as male, but this is solely because my image of female has been so disturbed by the messages of Christianity and incest that it seems unbelievable to conceive of myself as made in God's image. I have not heard the message 'You are made in the image of God'. Neither my church or family value me as made in God's image – they didn't say or believe I was, so it is now difficult to believe I am. This is slowly changing but remains a struggle.

Some survivors cannot perceive God as male. One survivor said 'You become instinctively afraid of Jesus because he's a man. "Father" for me is the most frightening name for God I can possibly think of'. She continued, 'Even though part of me is still scared of God because of the masculine I am determined not to let anyone rob me of my relationship with Him. I look in the scriptures for other images of God – like God is light and shelter, spirit, wind and water.'

Our image of God and of ourselves is only one problem among many for us Christian survivors. Much pain and anger stems also from the silence of the church on sexual abuse. There is no condemnation from the pulpits, no liturgies of support and compassion, no prayers or sermons. The church has simply crossed to the other side of the road in the dubious tradition of the religious leaders in the parable of the Good Samaritan. Even today when sexual abuse receives considerable media attention, the majority of ministers and seminary students know almost nothing about the dynamics of sexual abuse, neither does the Christian community.

The church tries to perpetuate this silence by asking survivors themselves to do something about it! They offer the survivors a tasty little spiritual pill which hopefully will take the 'headache' away – the pill – the admonition to 'forgive and forget'. All the women in my Christian Survivors group have been told to 'forgive and forget'. Forgiving and forgetting is seen as the way 'Good people' behave regardless of the fact that it can be pathological and dangerous advice for those who have suffered abuse. This misbegotten advice has led many survivors to bury deep within themselves the experiences that deprived them of their dignity. Asking survivors to 'forgive and forget' is one way of not addressing the real suffering and pretending the abuse never happened. The abuse can never be forgotten and should not be forgotten. How is it we so quickly ask survivors to forgive and forget and never ask for justice for the survivor? When we are asked to forgive, no one mentions our violation or the responsibility for repentance and restitution from the abuser. They hand back to us the responsibility and when we say we find it difficult (or impossible) to forgive and forget they load on more guilt by pointing the finger at us and saying 'See – a bad and sinful woman'.

We are told that anger is not a Christian virtue, that the more extravagant emotions do not belong in church – melancholy, tears, fear, anxiety, panic, urgency, deep need and insecurity. This is why I have chosen the reading of Jesus going into the temple, angry and in a rage overturning the tables and benches and telling the people they have made his temple into a den of thieves. He was angry about the violation of His temple. We are angry about the violation of ours. This body of mine houses my soul, it is my temple, God's house, sacred and beautiful. I am angry that my temple has been violated and Jesus is too. But the church is not. At the beginning I said (or rather Mary Paullauer said) that ministry occurs when the skin of the soul is rubbed raw. Christian Survivors of Sexual Abuse – CSSA East London – was

born out of the rawness of my soul and the souls of other
Christian survivors.[1] It was born out of the rejection and silence
about our presence of our churches. Last weekend nine members
of CSSA (we are in touch with sixty Christian survivors) –
Anglican, Catholic and Baptist – went on Retreat. The Retreat
was led by an Anglican Deacon who was also a survivor of
childhood sexual abuse. It was an amazing, powerful and
wonderful experience. We asked the survivors at the end of the
weekend what they felt about the Retreat and what had happened
for them. They said '... a lot of crying' ... 'I felt understood
without having to explain'. These were just two of the comments.
In the absence of support and acceptance from our churches we
will support each other. Because of the silence of our churches we
will hear each other. Every two weeks we meet in East London
and this poem by Edwina Gateley called 'The Sharing' will give
you some idea of what our meetings are about.

> We told our stories –
> that's all
> We sat and listened to each other
> and heard the journeys of each soul.
> We sat in silence
> entering each one's pain and
> sharing each one's joy.
> We heard love's longing
> and the lonely reachings-out
> for love and affirmation.
> We heard of dreams shattered
> and visions fled
> of hopes and laughter
> turned stale and dark.
> We felt the pain of
> isolation and
> the bitterness of death.
>
> But in each brave and
> lonely story
> God's gentle life
> broke through.

[1] Christian Survivors of Sexual Abuse now at BM-CSSA, London
WC1N 3XX.

And we heard music in
the darkness
and smelt flowers
in the void.

We felt the budding of
creation
in the searching of
each soul.
And discerned the beauty
of God's hand in
each muddy, twisted path.

And his voice sang
in each story
his life sprang from
each death.
Our sharing became one story
of a simple lonely search
for life and hope and
oneness
in a world which sobs
for love.
And we knew that in
our sharing
God's voice with
mighty breath
was saying
love each other and take each other's hand.

For you are one
though many
and in each of you
I live.
So listen
to my story
and share my pain
and death
oh listen to my story
and rise and live
with me.[2]

---

[2] Edwina Gateley, 'The Sharing', *Sounds of a Lay Woman*, A. Clarke 1988.

We listen to each other. In our group we affirm the value of each other and last weekend, on Retreat, we made flowers and offered them to one another. This is the flower given to me. It was given to me by our youngest Christian Survivor. She writes on the back: 'Dear Margaret, Thank you for the Retreat and for the group, it's a life saver!' She adds a quotation from Isaiah 49: 'Even if a mother forgets her baby, I will never forget you. Look I've branded you on the palm of my hands'. 'Margaret – I think you're great! May God give you courage and strength and hope and peace of life.' I cried. Because I felt loved and valued. We really want as Christian Survivors of Sexual Abuse to be able to say of our Christian communities, and to say it with love and gratitude:

> I was raped and you stood by me.
> I was beaten and you sheltered me.
> I was abused and you intervened.
> I was in pain and you comforted me.
> I was orphaned and you mothered me.
> I was confused and you brought me insight.
> I was silent and you listened to me.
> I was seeking and you searched with me.
> I was knocking and you opened the door.[3]

We are alive, we are present in your midst. We are not going to be secret Christian Survivors. Secrecy is hurting us badly. Telling us to 'forgive and forget', and not be angry, is not enough. It's too simplistic. Justice and healing become the responsibility of the whole Christian community; it is not just our responsibility. As Edwina Gateley's poem said

> So listen to my story
> and share my pain
> and death
> oh listen to my story
> and rise and live
> with me.

[3] Mary Pellauer, *Sexual Assault and Abuse: A Handbook for Clergy and Religious Professionals*, HarperCollins 1991.

Margaret Kennedy

ON THE JOURNEY TOGETHER*

Luke 1.39–45; 24.13–34

Feet and hands: These are the symbols I offer as we think about journeying together.

FEET – to stand for the moving-on that our faith demands of us, HANDS – to stand for the togetherness, the companionship, the support most of us need, and may legitimately seek, as we set out in response to the promptings of the Spirit.

Feet and hands were involved in Mary's journey into the hill country to see her cousin Elizabeth.

Elizabeth was older than Mary: until recently, she had journeyed through her life feeling unfulfilled because – while Jewish culture required married women to be mothers – she had borne no children. And now, when she had good cause to lay aside all hope, she was pregnant with John, who was to be the forerunner of Christ.

Mary, on the other hand, was young and pregnant. But she was *un*married and Jewish culture frowned upon – in fact legislated against – pregnancy out of wedlock. The penalty for a pregnancy when the father was someone other than the betrothed man could be death by stoning.

So although, as we know, Mary had placed her trust in God, she would have been conscious of the possibility of human censure: she journeyed to see Elizabeth no doubt feeling something of the reproach that her cousin, for different reasons, had felt for many years. But I guess she also felt excited and full of joy and wonder – on both her own and Elizabeth's account. She went so that experiences of both men's reproach and God's blessing could be shared. She went so that hands could be held out in sisterly (or cousinly) support.

And both women – the young one and the older one – found what they were looking for in this get-together: the affirmation of their worth and of the new roles they'd undertaken, encourage-

* A sermon for the Women's World Day of Prayer, March 1991.

ment to follow God's leading, and a joyful sense of commitment
that burst out in hymns recognizing the value God places on those
whom society underrates. It is possible, since Mary visited
her cousin in the sixth month of Elizabeth's pregnancy and stayed
for three months, that she helped Elizabeth through labour and
birth – when the outstretched and supportive hands of another
woman are so welcome. This would be a practical, incarnational
(embodied) expression of the emotional and spiritual support
that clearly flowed between the two women.

And then we move from before the birth of Jesus to a point
after his death and resurrection, to consider another journey: that
of Cleopas and his companion on the road from Jerusalem to
Emmaus. We don't know for sure who the companion was, but as
they shared a house, it may be fair to assume that they were
husband and wife: John, in his Gospel, mentions that one of the
women at the foot of the cross was Mary, wife of Clopas. Possibly
Clopas and Cleopas were one and the same. It doesn't matter
greatly. The point is that here were two people who, in grief and
disillusionment, shared a journey that was transformed by the
drawing near and companionship of a third traveller – the one
they finally recognized as Jesus himself. Thinking everything
they'd hoped for was over, they'd been going back home ... back
to resume life where they'd left it off – much as Peter sadly
reckoned he might as well go back to his fishing. But something
happened to change the pace and direction of their feet, and the
lift of their hands: one imagines that where, on the way to
Emmaus, their feet had been slow and dragging and their hands
supporting each other in shared agony, the return journey (verse
33: They got up *at once* and went *back* to Jerusalem) was marked
by running feet and hands held out in shared joy. For between the
agony and the joy were the hands of one who took bread,
blessed, broke and gave – and, in that familiar action, told them
everything they longed to know.

Now – Jewish faith, Christian faith, many faiths – have from
time immemorial likened the spiritual life to a journey. I think it
was William Barclay who used to begin each day, even if he were
going to spend all of it in his study, by putting on his walking
boots. Some of the contemplative disciplines that interest so
many people nowadays include walking meditations ... giving

attention to the rhythm of raising and lowering the feet – much as breathing meditations help us to be attentive to the rhythm of inhalation and exhalation. The walking meditation points up for us, not only the need for a journeying mentality, but also an approach to spirituality which is holistic, which involves the body as well as the psyche. It reminds us that spiritual opening-out only happens when we are prepared to move constantly from fixed ideas, old prejudices and the safety of the familiar into the beckoning territory of God's kingdom – and when we do so with the *whole person*. So the symbol of *feet* reminds us that the Christian life is a journeying life – not in any way a new idea, though something about which we need to keep reminding ourselves.

But what I find particularly refreshing in the emphasis of this theme is the *hands* part ... the togetherness bit ... the suggestion that the spiritual journey we're all called to make is properly a process of sharing and mutual support.

Western spirituality has largely stressed the *feet* part of the equation at the expense of the *hands*. It's been assumed that each of us has to make our journey towards God on our own. Reading the literature of spirituality, there's a kind of solitary, lonesome, 'I did it my way' tint to it all. Most of the saints seem to have had disciples rather than friends.

But maybe the *tint* is actually a *taint*. Maybe there's a serious deficiency in the rather macho idea of going it alone. For God is not just *my* God but, as the Lord's prayer has it, *our* God. I grow more and more convinced that true spirituality is not about finding one's own individual peace, and saving one's own individual soul: rather, it's about finding one's connectedness with others, and working towards the wholeness of all. It's finding God in the *journey*, rather than simply in the destination ('I am the *Way*', said Jesus) – and God is in the down-to-earth companionship with others on the road as well as at the end of the trail.

This is an emphasis I find much more true to my experience as a woman than the solitary ladder-climbing picture of the spiritual journey. Not too many women have the freedom – or even perhaps the desire – to go it alone and 'do it my way', regardless of others. Most of us have (or have had) family or other caring responsibilities: we bleed, we sweat, we cry for others, we have to

take the wishes of others into account all the time: if this
supporting role isn't born in us, it's certainly bred in us ... we *feel*
connected: we don't really feel anything like Bunyan's Christian
who could just drop everything and toddle off on his own. Our
spiritual journey has to be made, and God has to be found, within
a network of human relationships, within the bodily, within the
down to earth and the everyday ...

And I think this is a strength, not a weakness. I think the
connectedness women feel with others – and indeed with the
earth, the elements and the body – is something wholly positive
that we can offer to spirituality today ... indeed, to social and
political life as a whole – in a world where 'I did it my way' can be
ultimately very dangerous. For the solitary journey, the journey
whose only concern is my soul, can lead into a disconnectedness
and a divorce from others and from our surroundings: it leads
into that unhealthy situation where we split apart spirit and body,
spirit and community, spirit and politics, spirit and environment,
spirit and ordinary life ... It is this splitting, I believe, that lies
behind men's attempt to sort out problems by violent means and
by war – an attempt that is also responsible for the rape of the
environment. It's a position that leads into one-way roads, to
extreme positions and confrontation – where openness, understanding and co-operation would better serve the purposes of
God.

So – feet certainly: we must use those. But let's also, as women,
have our offering of hands ... in other words, let's offer our
insights and our example about the necessity for supportiveness,
connectedness, togetherness ... in this poor fragmented and
fragile world.

As we make our journey, let's stress 'harambee' (a Kenyan
word that literally means 'pulling together') ... 'harambee' in
pain, 'harambee' in joy, 'harambee' as we seek and find God in
the everyday, and in each other.

T. Rayner has written:[1]

Will you walk with me,
Shall we share together on our journey?

You and I will follow Jesus and his saints,
Looking for their footsteps clearly planted in the earth,

Watching their way over hard rock,
Listening for their words of encouragement
When the way seems hard;
Taking the outstretched hand of help ...

More than that;
On a journey such as ours
Each can be alongside the other.
Jesus himself walks at our side,
Sharing each joy or sorrow,
Saving us from falling over stones and potholes.
You and I will be his hands and heart for the others.

Will you walk with me?

[1]   In the *Anthology* produced for the Women's World Day of Prayer 1991, edited by E. Birch.

Kate Compston

SHAME

Luke 8.40–56

I want to talk about miracles. Luke's gospel tells two beautiful stories of something miraculous happening – the healing of the woman with the haemorrhage, and the raising of Jairus's daughter. I sometimes find it difficult to think about miracles, or to feel entirely comfortable with them because one part of my mind, the sensible,rational, scientific part wants to say, this is just a figure of speech, things like that don't really happen, while the other part of my mind, the part that senses that there's more to this than meets the eye, the part that just has a gut feeling about all sorts of things, wants to come a little closer, get a little nearer to that curious feeling. And, rather than struggle with these mixed feelings, sometimes its easier just to avoid them altogether.

So, we know that if someone has a haemorrhage, or at least

something like a continual menstrual period that went on for years, even weeks, nowadays it would be treated by doctors who might well put her on the pill to regulate her bleeding. And we would probably surmise that Jairus's daughter was in some kind of coma or catatonic sleep. Different times, different medical knowledge. But we have the same emotions, the same fears, the same experience of being human. Let's try to get a little closer to that experience of humanness.

And we have to have a little background knowledge here. The woman with the flow of blood didn't just have an inconvenient, debilitating and possibly painful physical condition. Under Jewish law, a menstruating woman was ritually unclean. That meant that she couldn't go to church – important when the whole of your country's life stems from and revolves round religion. But even worse, it meant that she made anyone who came in contact with her unclean too. So of course, people kept well away from her, isolated her, put her in a kind of quarantine. She would have to live separately, sleep separately, eat from different dishes. She would be starved of human contact. And on top of all that, there was the whole stigma and shame of feeling unclean, of knowing that you would contaminate everyone who came in contact with you. Essentially, she had become an outcast from her community, hateful to herself and everyone else. That was bearable, perhaps for one week in four, when you were like other women. But twelve years!

Does it sound barbaric? Think again. Have you ever had the experience of something that made you feel shut off from all the brightness and hope of everyday life? Perhaps you've been disablingly ill, and have felt isolated from the community of strong, healthy people who seem to have so much energy, so many choices, and you imagine that people are pitying you, or you're just a nuisance, that you're no use to anyone or anything. Or perhaps you've been depressed, locked in a kind of dark prison, shut away from the community of cheerful, purposeful people who, you think, can't possibly understand what it's like. Have you ever been made redundant or had a long period of unemployment, excluded from the community of people with jobs, money, prospects, status, while you feel unwanted, only fit for the scrapheap or the dole? Or perhaps there is a lot of pain for you in your sexual orientation or behaviour; you're afraid to be yourself, unsure, with a thousand messages about your unacceptability running through your mind. Or it's that you've done something you feel very bad about, something that fills you with guilt and horror, that excludes you from the community of good people. Or maybe its simply that you've been deeply hurt or rejected by someone you care about. There are so many ways of feeling oneself to be excluded, shut out, unworthy, unclean, outcast. We can each name our own shame, our own exclusion zone, in imagination if not in reality.

And that shame, that exclusion, that uncleanness becomes like a haemorrhage, draining all our confidence, all our sense of self-worth, of being people who matter in some way. Hope and joy and freedom seep away like a never-ending flow of blood. And the more it goes on, the more we loathe ourselves, and assume that everyone else must also find us loathsome. It's a vicious circle. The less we can feel at home with ourselves, the less confidence we have to reach out to other people – and the worse we feel about ourselves – and the worse we feel about them. And the harder it is for others to be with us, not because of how *they* feel but because our relations with them have become distorted.

When we get into that state, we tend to find that one of two things is likely to happen. Either we withdraw completely into ourselves, become more and more wrapped up in our own misery until we become pretty indifferent to others. Or we attack as a form of defence, we hurt people before they can hurt us, we are on guard. And of course, in this state, it's fatally easy to imagine all kinds of unreal things about other people. We imagine they're talking about us, laughing at us, pitying us in a demeaning kind of way; that they don't care or understand how we feel. We imagine that *they* think we're unclean, not worth bothering about. And the awful thing is that sometimes, our imagining is real. People and organizations and governments and countries *do* behave like that sometimes, they *are* exclusive, they do treat people as if they don't matter. And it's as well to recognize that fact, and to name the exclusion. Because when it happens, it often requires considerable determination, considerable courage, not to accept it or go along with it.

But it's not the whole story. Not everybody is like that, and not all the time. The truth is, we all do it sometimes. We all exclude people sometimes, often without even realizing, and we do it for all sorts of reasons, many of which we are not responsible for. It's just what we were taught to do. But one of the saddest things about the awful cycle of hurt and exclusion and shame and anger is that it makes judgment very unreliable and forgiveness very hard.

It's this whole mess of blame and guilt and separation and bad judgment and fear and loathing and the voices that haunt us from the past saying ... you don't fit ... you're not wanted ... get lost ... that the Bible calls sin. Sin is living out of our fears. Sin is not being free. It's the seepage of our whole sense of ourselves. It's feeling like the woman with the haemorrhage of blood. I imagine that she might have felt something like this:

Shame, or not shame.
I never know.
I know that all the messages of flesh
and blood scream at me, 'shame, you should feel shame,
you are not clean, you do not measure up
to what the standard is.'
This seepage, slippage, flow and flood,
this blood that comes and comes
but will not come in proper places
but shames and blames and bleeds
upon the rags of pride and shame
and stains and taints and taunts
and shames and haunts the wretchedness
of those who claim, or would absorb it.
This blood, that I cannot contain
that rises, swells, torments, distends,
that weakens, wastes, defeats, unsexes,
undermines and unacceptably lays low,
this shame, this means that never finds an end,
this blood, this flood, this torrent never spent,
this shame, this shame, this shame.

But shame is not the end of the story. Or it needn't be. Like the woman, perhaps there is something else, some instinct, some deep desire or belief, even some despair, that says, ever so quietly ...

'this isn't true. *This is not true.* THIS IS NOT THE WAY IT'S MEANT TO BE. *THIS IS A LIE.*' That small voice haunts us, drives us, to take a risk, to reach out, to touch just the hem of a cloak, to claim back our humanity, our belonging, our life, to put an end to fear. That small voice is the voice of God! The woman who touched Jesus's cloak took a terrible risk. Not only was she an outcast. By touching him, she made him unclean too – and he was a rabbi, a teacher – a man! No wonder that she tried to do it secretly, no wonder that she trembled when she was discovered. But she heard the voice of God – and she acted:

And yet,
there is a deeper thing than even blood
that growls within my soul and surges
as the urge of shame is shy to do,
and roars exultant, trembling, fearful of its ower.

I WILL TOUCH
I WILL CLAIM
I WILL END

After all,
this too is human,
this too is true.
If human is acceptably
what I am, or you, or you,
then I am this,
and this is human,
and there is no shame
in being this.
And this is, shameless, touching, who I am!

Jesus treated no one as unclean. Not lepers, not bleeding women, not tax collectors, or publicans, not adulterers, not soldiers or criminals, not foreigners nor the mentally ill, not drunks or prostitutes, not the dead. But even Jesus had to make the journey which led him to that point. In the fifteenth chapter of Matthew's Gospel, we find him rejecting the notion that it is external attitudes, circumstances, behaviour, that renders a person unclean. Uncleanness cannot be imposed from without. Rather, it is the hateful, prideful and covetous intentions of the heart that taint and corrupt human behaviour. And yet, immediately after, his own words judge even Jesus, in his encounter with the Syro-Phoenician woman, who comes to him seeking healing for her daughter, and is spoken to by Jesus in a way that today would be actionable under the Race Relations Act. But she answers with humility and determination – and Jesus, in his turn, has the humility to recognize the extent of her faith, and the insight to learn something very important from her. From this point onward, he dismisses or denigrates no one, and his mission is enlarged still further, beyond the familiar circle of his own people and culture.

This openness continually led Jesus to break the rules of who was out and who was in, who was unclean and who was not. He saw that they were human rules, made by people who were so fearful that they needed to control rather than live by trust, needed to make others appear unclean in order to reinforce their own cleanness, their own justification. He saw, and lived out the belief that God's way was something quite other. God's way was one of passionate, unconditional love, that did not depend on what people had done or not done, but continually sought human wellbeing and right relationship. It was a way which offered forgiveness instead of self-justification, responsibility instead of victimization, love instead of fear and freedom instead of shame.

All the time, there are people around us who reach out to touch us, to make contact, to be reassured that they matter, that they count, that they need not be ashamed of being the unique, God-created people they are. We can let them touch us. The cost of letting them touch us, and there is a cost, is not so high as the cost of being untouchable. Because this is an activity of mutuality. The extent to which we allow ourselves to be touched by others is the extent to which we in turn are able to touch in our own need. We don't need to agree with them, or pretend that we approve of their actions if we don't. Acceptance does not preclude the demands of justice. Nor do they need to be the same kind of people as us. We can let them be different. Jesus simply was attentive to people, gave an assurance of utter respect and worth to bleeding and humiliated people which set *them* free to let go of their victimized or oppressive ways. And we can resist structures and laws which exclude or dehumanize. H.A. Williams once described miracles as 'experienced resurrection'. Jesus raised people up, from their backs, from their knees, and on to their feet. And he pushed on to their own two feet those who were standing with their feet on the necks of the poor. And he congratulated and affirmed those people whose faith was so strong that, against all the odds, they stood up themselves.

That kind of miracle, of experienced resurrection, is there when we are ready to take the risk and endure the pain of reaching out to be raised into new life, of being set free from the shame of the past, of other people's unkindness and unforgiveness and of our own. Jesus said to the woman with the haemorrhage not, go in peace, I have healed you, but, go in peace, your own faith has made you well. And he said to Jairus and his family – don't cry, she is not dead, she is only sleeping. He saw with the sight of God-people living out of their freedom and not out of their fears. This offered possibility is cause for gratitude.

You suffered me,
allowed me,
let me touch you,
confirmed me,
authorized my own authority,
permitted me my being,
let me claim that knowledge
which reluctance, fear, or just the shock of boldness
relegated to the silent shadows of my heart,
substantiated it.
Oh, but more,
you honoured it.

You did not turn away, repelled,
condemn or threaten or excuse.
You did not abort, curtail, or clear your throat.
It was not you – I did it, touched you,
made an end to fear, though fearfully I did it...
I am made whole.
I think it cost you – yes, of course it would.
For this I offer no apologies.

You paid it with a smile.
Such is the price of love,
for you as well as me.
You paid it with a smile.

I should go, get on,
there is so much to do,
and getting used to living without bleeding
will take some practice.
But I want to spend a few more minutes
savouring the taste of shamelessness
and the fierce delight that lies the other side
of wounded pride.

You suffered me.
I knew you would.
I had faith in you.

Kathy Galloway

SATURDAY NIGHTS

Isaiah 25.6–9; Matthew 8.5–17

On Saturday nights, if we're free, Chris and I enter the Kingdom of Heaven. We get an excellent piece of steak, open a bottle of red wine, and accept God's invitation to dine. After that, we settle down to a little reproduction – the copying of the church notices, that is.

The invitation to dine at the table of life is all over the pages of the Bible. I might have used as a reading from the Hebrew scriptures part of the otherwise rather stark book of Proverbs, in which the Wisdom of God is shown as a woman luring young men to enter her house, using all the blandishments at her disposal. We might have read that she sets up a house, sends out her agents into the streets to call people in: 'Come, eat the

food that I have prepared and taste the wine that I have spiced'
(Prov. 9.5).

We read from the prophet Isaiah, 'On this mountain Yahweh
Sabaoth will prepare a banquet of rich food for all peoples, a
banquet of wines well matured, the best of meats and the finest of
wines.' So there it is. The banquet is ready for us, and for all
peoples. No one is to be excluded. Let everybody come. This is the
invitation to the Kingdom of Heaven, to the new creation, to
participate in the joys of heaven, not after death, but here, in this
life.

Jesus called it, 'life in all its fullness', and he offered it, and
offers it now, to those who follow him.

Look at the way people's lives were changed when they met
Jesus. Matthew's Gospel tells of the household of Simon Peter,
struck by illness when his mother-in-law was disabled by fever,
unable to take any active part in life. Almost as a footnote, the
writer records the healing of this nameless woman, and her
restoration to family life. After her, they brought to him many
people with all kinds of illness, to be healed.

Matthew notes that this was the fulfilment of a famous passage
from Isaiah 53, from the great solemn poem about the suffering
servant. But it was also the practical demonstration of what Jesus
himself had just said: 'I tell you, many will come from the east and
west to sit with Abraham, Isaac and Jacob at the banquet in the
kingdom of heaven.'

The invitation goes out: people respond, and come in to find
that the banquet is real. The new creation is here. The message of
the hell-fire preachers used to be that the Kingdom of Heaven is
nigh – as a kind of warning! Prepare to meet thy God! Yes, indeed
the Kingdom of Heaven is nigh, nigher than they thought – but
the warning is – beware that you don't miss the feast.

Jesus was like profligate Wisdom, flinging open the doors to all
comers (John 7.37). He welcomed people who were outside most
people's reckoning.

He travelled with a company of women disciples – a shocking
piece of behaviour in any society, and even more in societies such
as Judea of the time, where a small culture was hanging on to
religious and moral purity against all the odds. He even
welcomed women who were known to have flouted the moral

code of the day: the Samaritan woman (John 4.1 ff.), the woman who wept all over his feet and dried them with her hair – I'd love to try that! You can hear the indignation ruffling through the Pharisee's voice: 'If this man were a prophet, he would know who is touching him (*touching!*) and what kind of woman she is!' (Luke 7.37).

And do you remember the story of the woman who was caught committing adultery? How the gleeful crowd brought her to Jesus. Here was a chance to catch him out. Surely in a clear case like this, he would have to condemn, to exclude. And he did – he invited the judges, possibly including the man with whom she was – we hear nothing of his condemnation, to consider their own fitness for the feast (John 4.1ff.).

No time or place was too sacred. He healed on the sabbath, and cried out the invitation from the steps of the Temple. No one was unworthy: the leper, the tax collector, the foreigner, the pig farmer, all heard the invitation, all responded, and their lives were radically altered.

Think of the centurion in Matthew's story. He knew that he was an outcast to most of the people of Israel at that time. He said to Jesus, 'I am not worthy to have you under my roof'. He was a gentile, and part of the occupying army, but none of that mattered. What mattered was the sickness of his servant, which Jesus could surely deal with without confronting all the prejudices and bitterness of the time.

Jesus did heal the servant. But he did not shy away from the issue of exclusion. Many times he was accused of offering the invitation, through healing or through his teaching, to people who were considered unsuitable to enter. Here he rounds on his accusers, and makes the theological point: 'I tell you, many will come from the east and west to sit with Abraham, Isaac and Jacob at the banquet in the Kingdom of Heaven' – you're going to have to get used to this!

And there's more. If the invitation is open to a lot of foreigners and sinners whom you would like to see shut out, it is open to the religious only on the same grounds. No one is guaranteed a place by birth, just as no one is excluded by birth. 'But those who were born to the Kingdom will be thrown out into the dark.'

The worst sin was not transgression of social or moral rules. The *worst* sin, the one thing which called forth all Jesus' scorn against the Pharisees, was refusing the invitation, and keeping others out too. He calls them 'hypocrites' (actors – playing a part), who 'make up heavy loads and pile them on the shoulders of others, but will not lift a finger to help them (Matt. 23.4), and accuses them: 'You shut the door of the Kingdom of Heaven in people's faces; you do not enter yourselves, and when others try to enter, you stop them' (Matt. 23.13).

The invitation is still open. People are entering the community of the new creation, the company of the Kingdom of Heaven, and others are still steadfastly keeping them out.

Recently, a friend who works for a homelessness project spent some time living rough. He found that he began to look like the homeless people he was living with, and to smell like them. One day, he said to the group who'd befriended him, 'Here, let's go to church'. They went, a group of scruffy, slightly pungent young men, to the church door at the beginning of the service, and were turned away. The door was shut in their face. The invitation was not given. Like the Pharisees, those earnest, religious church-goers shut the door of the Kingdom of Heaven, and didn't realise that it was they who were on the outside.

But that's too obvious and easy an example. There are countless and complex ways for us to slam that door in people's faces, considering ourselves safe on the inside, when, in reality, we are out in the cold, and keeping others out.

When Chris and I sit down to our rich repast on a Saturday night, our luxury depends on a structure of injustice which is keeping the majority of the world's population outside, hungry and downtrodden. We cannot but be aware of the homeless population of our part of Islington, shut outside our cosy comfort, dependent on the hand-outs we give. And in the flats and bedsits, and perhaps in the big houses too, lonely, embittered people are excluded from the warmth of human love which makes our meal into a celebration.

Maybe we shouldn't do it. Should we turn ascetic? Refrain from the real pleasures of love, companionship, food and drink? Because others are kept outside, should we stay outside ourselves, as a matter of principle – a sort of inverse Pharisaism? No. Hang on. It's all too easy to make a luxury of guilt. Well then, perhaps the feast should be regarded as eschatological, or purely spiritual – this, after all, is the theology of the Victorian age, which reconciled people to great present suffering with the promise of good things to come hereafter. Perhaps if our social climate is returning to the Victorian age, our theology should follow.

But neither the voluntary misery of the ritual fast, nor quietism today, with the promise of future rewards, is the way of Jesus, or the great prophets of the Hebrew people. Physical pleasures are many, and are vigorously celebrated in scripture. The response to people's exclusion from their enjoyment is not a shrinking from pleasure, but an equally robust prophetic anger against the forces that hamper and the systems that oppress.

Nobody knows what order the writings known to us as the book of Isaiah originally had. But much later on in Isaiah as we have it in our Bibles, the prophet describes the way life is to be in this new community. It isn't fasting that God wants, but justice – to remove the fetters of injustice and set free those who are oppressed (Isa.58.6). In this way the new community, the new creation will be built, in which God and the people of God share delight in each other; in which lives are strong and free, work is rewarded with its true dignity, and the peace which binds the human community will flow over into all creation (Isa. 65.17–25).

This new creation, begun in Jesus and continued in our lives, is to be a glorious affront to all that hampers fullness of life. It is a celebration of love confronting the world with its bitterness and hate; a delight in creation confronting the world with its rapacity; sheer enjoyment at the feast confronting the world with its dourness and its greed.

If the door to the Kingdom of Heaven opens wide enough to let you in, and me in, then all who will may enter. It means having the courage to embrace people and causes that are distasteful to our world, to speak out and act against all who would kill joy and maim delight, even, let it be said, if they end up killing and maiming us.

The love that calls is the love that Jesus showed, the love that heals and welcomes people who are damaged and abused, just as we are being welcomed and healed, re-created and restored.

OK. There is the invitation. The table is laid, the feast is ready. Let's go in.

Janet Woolton

ON THE DEATH OF A BABY

Psalm 139.1–18, 23, 24

When we look in the Bible to find passages that speak about God's love, we may automatically turn first to the New Testament, particularly the Gospels. But we must not overlook the Old Testament, for we see there too how God loved and cared for people, and how his loving power was at work in their lives.

Psalm 139 speaks very clearly about God's knowledge and care, and about his presence with us, wherever we are. It speaks about God's presence and love at the very beginning of life, even within the womb. I have turned to this Psalm many times over the last few years, and its message has been very dear to me as I experienced pregnancy and parenthood.

My husband, Ian, and I have two daughters, Naomi and Hannah. We also have a son, Benjamin, who died the day after he was born.

Benjamin was born at twenty-eight weeks gestation, by Caesarian Section, on 21 April 1982. I had severe pre-eclampsia – a serious complication of pregnancy which leads to raised blood pressure and kidney problems. I had been on bed rest and medication for two weeks, but as I was not responding to this treatment, the birth had to be brought forward.

Benjamin weighed 2lb 9oz at birth. He was taken to the Special Care Baby Unit, and for a while he breathed spontaneously. However, he began to have difficulty in breathing, and the following day he was put on a ventilator. His condition deteriorated rapidly, and he died a few hours later. I was taken to Special Care very quickly when we realized he was dying, but, sadly, I was not in time to see him alive, nor to guide him through death.

As I held Benjamin for the first and last time, I was strongly aware of God's presence. God was not far off, not just looking on. God was there, with us, and had been there throughout the six months of Benjamin's life in the womb, and throughout Benjamin's short life after birth. God was there too in Benjamin's death, and was with us in our tears. God was there in our rejoicing in being part of the creation of this beautiful child, and God was there in our sorrow over his death. If anyone knew what I was going through, surely it must be God, because God's own son died too.

I clung on to that awareness, and to the hope that I would see Benjamin again. Sometimes, in the midst of the pain and the grief and the tears, the awareness of God's presence and the belief in life after death were the only things that made any kind of sense. My world had been turned upside down. I had lost my sense of identity; I was a parent, yet not a parent. How could I be a parent without a child? My expectations, my plans for the future, had been snatched away.

Babies are not supposed to die. We expect to outlive our parents. We don't expect to have to plan our child's funeral. Nobody talks about it. And when it happens, parents are not expected, or allowed, to grieve, at least not for very long. For some reason, many people think that because the child was so young, the parents will not grieve much. Yet mental health professionals and counsellors (not to mention bereaved parents) recognize that bereavement following the death of a baby or young child may be the most difficult bereavement of all to cope with.

After Benjamin's death, I grieved, for a long time. At first I failed to recognize the fact that I was grieving. When I did recognize it, I pushed it away. I was afraid of my grief; I didn't know how to handle it. Nobody else seemed to know either. Very few people would talk about it. They seemed afraid of it too. When I couldn't push it away any longer, I ran away from it. But in the end, I found that it caught up with me. Finally, I had to face it, and deal with it. And so I found that I had to start grieving again, several years later.

And that was very painful. It was almost more than I could bear to go back to the beginning and start again. Yet I came to realize that this was the only way forward. And with Ian's help, with the help of professionals and that of a very good friend, I was guided through my grief. First, I had to go back, to re-live the days of Benjamin's life. By looking at his medical records, I was able to learn more about him, to regain the hours that I had lost through being ill and sedated after the delivery. At last, I was able to celebrate the fact that he had lived. Then, I had to move on, beyond his life, and face the fact that he had died. I was helped to trace his grave, and have his name inscribed on the headstone. When that was complete, I felt a great sense of peace. Here at last was public ackowledgment that I had had a son; that he had existed; that he had lived, and that he had died.

It was accomplished.

And so, in one sense, that is the end. But in another sense, it never can be the end.

Is there an end to grieving? I'm not sure. There comes a time when we can cope with the pain of grief, when we can carry our grief and it no longer carries us, but I don't think it ever really comes to an end.

Is there an end to the sadness? Not really. I don't think I shall ever again experience the pure joy I felt during my pregnancy with Benjamin. The pain does come less often, but when it does it may come with the same intensity.

Is there ever an end to the loving? No. Benjamin was my child, a very precious first born son. I loved him, before he was born, and after. His death does not put an end to that love. I can understand more fully now that love is stronger than death.

So where can we expect to get to in our grief if the pain and sadness never completely go away? Can we hope for acceptance of the death? That is hard. Can I realistically ever hope to accept Benjamin's death, when it came so quickly after his birth, so suddenly, before he had a proper chance of life? If accepting it means believing 'it was for the best' or that 'it was God's will', then no, I cannot accept it.

Can we get to the point of 'letting go'? I am not sure what this means. Does it mean letting go of the pain and the grief? If so, I don't know how to do that or whether I can, or even, paradoxically, if I want to. The pain and the grief I feel are an expression of the love I have for Benjamin. I don't want that to be taken away. Are we, then, to 'let go' of the person who has died? Again, I'm not sure what that means. I don't know how to 'let go' of someone I had for so brief a time. If it involves forgetting what happened, putting it behind me, I cannot do it, and think it quite wrong to attempt it. How can I forget my child? How can I deny he existed? Benjamin enriched my life, and continues to do so. His life and death gave my ministry a clear direction, within the work of the Stillbirth and Neonatal Death Society. I carry him again within me in that work.

I believe I have now come to terms with Benjamin's death. I can now cope with my feelings of bereavement, and can feel at peace with the pain. Perhaps that is as much as I can expect. Perhaps that is as far as we can go in grief. Maybe I will never reach the point of accepting Benjamin's death. But I have reached the point of accepting the pain of grief. That is part of my life, and I recognize that it always will be. For me, that is part of parenthood. I have faced the pain, at last, and am no longer afraid of it.

I cannot let Benjamin go; but I have reached the stage in my grief where I can welcome him into my life, in spite of and through the pain, and I can allow him to take his place in our family, as a very much loved first born son, whose life and death helped me to learn more about myself, and about the meaning of love, which goes beyond death, and on into eternity.

When I read the accounts of Jesus' death and resurrection, I feel a great affinity with Mary, who went to the tomb early in the morning to anoint Jesus' body. She, like me, had not had time to say goodbye properly to the one she loved; she longed to touch him, caress him, hold him, once more, before she prepared his body for burial. She wanted to cling to him, to hold on to him; she could not let him go.

But she was sent out, to tell the good news of love's triumph over evil, of life's victory over death.

Like Mary, I can now believe more fully in life after death. In life, Benjamin gave me so much; that lives on after his death. And I have come to see that there is life, for me, after his death.

And if that is real for me, I am called to make it real for other
people who are grieving for someone they love.
Like Mary, I too have a gospel to proclaim.

Benjamin, 'son of my right hand',
our first born.
Through you I learnt how precious life is
and yet how fragile.
Tiny, fragile, precious, I loved you.
I ached for you in your struggle to live.
You lost the battle and, in a way, so did I.
For you were part of me once.
You and I, completely one.
The parting came too soon for you,
and for me.
The parting which should have been a beginning
was but an end.

Tiny, fragile, precious, I loved you.

You lost the earthly battle;
but the parting, though an end for me,
was but a beginning for you –
a beginning of love, far greater and deeper than any love
I could have given you.

Through you I learnt how precious life is.
Through you I knew joy,
complete and un-utterable joy, welling up inside me,
causing me to proclaim your beauty
as I held you for the first and last time.
For that joy
there is no end;
only a beginning.

Sarah Brewerton

THIS IS MY BODY

> Which of you by taking thought
> can add one cubit to her stature?

In hospital your body is not your own. You are weighed, measured, shaved, bathed, drugged, assaulted by scalpel, confined. It's a routine operation, they say cheerfully, in the face of your apprehension, your anxiety, your fear, your terror.

It may be routine to you, but this is my body. It's the only one I've got.

The anaesthetist turns out to be a quiet, reassuring figure. I'm glad. To be anaesthetized is terrifying. I know: it's happened to me before. You hand over your body, mind, will, thoughts, feelings, survival. For weeks I'd been unable to imagine any future beyond surgery, beyond anaesthesia. I'd feared it as if it were death. If this is a kind of dying, will there be any resurrection?

Coming round, waking up, resurrecting from the death of the conscious mind under anaesthetic, was a strange experience: first awareness was of bodily sensation – thirst and a full bladder. Neither of these could be rectified immediately, and until they could be, they dominated such foggy consciousness as I had. All the great important issues of life, all politics, all ideas all other priorities flee in the face of these stark physical questions: When can I have something to drink? When will my muscles remember how to empty my bladder?

And later on: How do I go about normal activities with a set of my abdominal muscles out of action? How do I get up off the bed or out of the bath? How is it that I have taken this body of mine so for granted, for so many years? It doesn't even look like my body: when I look down, what I see marching across my lower abdomen is a row of shiny metal clips, forming a raised ridge, looking like a zip-fastener holding me together. I feel fragile, vulnerable, as if that zip-fastener could open up and ... what? Reveal a vast void inside me? Display my hollowness, my emptiness, to the world, to myself? I tell myself not to be so silly. I know better than to think that there really is a hole inside me ... but the fantasy persists. They have taken my womb away, and what else could there possibly be in its place but a gaping hole?

The bed next to mine had been empty since the day I was admitted. Two days after my surgery, a young woman was brought in and put into that bed. Her young husband settled her in, and when visiting hours ended he said a reluctant goodbye and left. By that time I was walking about the ward as much as I could: we were encouraged to move about as it was 'good for our circulation'. I could see that she was tearful, walked over to her and asked how she was. She was miscarrying her first baby and was confined to bed. I made the right sympathetic noises; she wept a little, talked about it. Then she asked me what I was there for. I started to tell her that I'd just had a hysterectomy and was suddenly overwhelmed by the contrast between this woman in her early twenties, attempting to embark on her childbearing; and me, nearly forty and childless, and now without a womb: those were my childbearing years and I didn't use them for that. So we both wept together, in an unexpected way finding that our very different circumstances gave each of us an entry into understanding and empathizing with what the other was feeling at that moment.

A little later a nurse noticed that I was tearful and said cheerfully: 'Never mind, it's just the post-op blues.' But that seemed to miss the point: there is a time to weep and a time to laugh; a time to mourn and a time to dance; and this was definitely a time to weep and mourn – to mourn the part of me, of my body, that had been taken away from me and could never be returned; and the part of my life that had gone and could not be lived over again in a different way. Of course, not all the mourning was done on that day; but a process was started, of grieving and letting go and moving on. So that a time came when I could laugh again, and a time came when my body could dance again.

Throughout my stay in hospital that bed next to mine was used as a short-stay bed for emergency admissions – women came and went, for twelve or twenty-four or thirty-six hours at a time: a miscarriage, an incomplete miscarriage, a haemorrhage ... there were, I think, only four or five such women during the time I was there, but it felt like many more; it felt like a constant procession of bleeding women. An image formed in my mind of a line of women stretching back, back, back into evolutionary time; of women's bodies as organisms for the making of babies; and when something goes wrong with that process, women bleed. I thought of how many millions of our foremothers had bled to death because there was no knowledge of how to stop the bleeding; and of how many places there still are in the world where women bleed to death, not for lack of knowledge or skill, but for lack of the political will to bring adequate medical care to poor women.

And I looked at this line of women stretching back in time in my mind, and was sad and angry. I wanted to grieve and rage at the same time, that this is what women, and the females of all species, have risked and lived in order that there shall be future generations. Some weeks later, when I described this to a wise friend, she asked me: 'And did you feel part of that line?' In a strange way I did, even though I have never even attempted to bear children: as if the fate, or potential fate, of any one of those women were also mine; as if what happened to any of those women, in some way happened to me.

One inescapable feature of a gynaecological ward is that every woman there is there precisely *because* she is a woman. In my experience, this had a striking levelling effect, crossing boundaries of age, class and occupation (I can't speak about race here as it happened that all of the women in the ward during the time that I was there were White and British). I don't mean to imply that all differences between us miraculously disappeared. There were still some who sat in the day-room, smoked, talked and watched TV; and some who occupied our beds during the day, as the only 'personal space' we had, and read, listened to our personal radios, wrote letters, wrote in our Journals or sat quietly with our own thoughts. Aside from the women who were confined to their beds at any given time, and so had no choice in the matter, the two different groups were constituted largely along predictable class lines.

However, running through and beneath and alongside these differences was the stark fact that being subjected to invasive surgery had reduced us all, in some ways, to being *bodies*. And when we talked with each other, a large part of our conversation was about our bodies: when we were to be allowed out of bed, or told we *must* get out of bed and walk about; who had the worst abdominal wind pain; when we would be allowed to have our first bath after our operations (bliss!); how many days it would be before we could expect a normal bowel movement (bliss!); who would be the next to walk slowly out of the toilets, beaming and saying 'I did it!'; who was farting the most; whether we could bear to laugh at the endless stream of jokes we cracked about our bodies, or did it still hurt too much to laugh; what was the state of our stitches or clips (which surgeons preferred which methods of putting us back together – can I see yours? this is what mine look like); and – stitches or clips – when were they coming out and would it hurt?

Early in the morning on the seventh day, which was a Sunday, a nurse came to take my clips out. As those fearsome bits of metal were removed from my abdomen I looked down, and there was my body, all in one piece again. It was all me; it was all my skin; I wasn't being held together by something else. In seven days my body had mended its external protection. I had lain in bed, read, dozed, listened to music, eaten my meals, slept. Without any knowledge or intervention from my conscious mind, my body had performed this miracle.

A few hours later the Anglican chaplain came to the ward, dressed up in all his fancy gear, carrying the chalice and paten covered by embroidered cloths, and wanting to give communion, to say a prayer, to 'remind us it was Sunday'. But he was too late, and anyway I had no need of his magic words: the miracle had already happened. The bread I had been eating for the past seven days was already my body.

Pam Lunn

2

Speaking from the Edge

One of the most exciting aspects of producing this collection has been the impetus created for talk amongst women about their experience of preaching. Most of us have never had the opportunity to speak with other women about this public but intimate concern. In one such conversation a gifted woman preacher commented on the number of times she had been told that it was difficult to listen to a voice like hers in the pulpit. Other women reported that this had been a frequent experience for them too. Many remarks about pitch, volume, tone and being 'difficult to follow' were shared. Amidst much laughter the group concluded that perhaps the most regular feedback they had received as preachers had been 'I'm sorry I find it difficult to hear/understand what you are trying to say'.

No doubt many male preachers would, on occasion, receive similar comments but the number of times they had been told that women's voices are difficult to listen to had convinced this group that the phrase expressed something very significant about the experience of preaching as a woman. It seemed to resonate with their conviction that it was not simply a problem of audibility that was being articulated but rather one concerning communication. People appear to find it difficult to hear those who are usually silent in public places, to take seriously speakers and concerns which are often marginalized and to contemplate the re-ordering of convictions that would be necessary if alternative perspectives were delivered from that most authoritative of settings – the pulpit.

In recent years feminist scholarship has devoted a good deal of attention to the problem of the speaking woman. Why is it that her words are often regarded as babble or hysteria? Why is it that they are uttered, but seem uncomprehensible and go unrecorded?

What subversive or radical potential is there to be found in speaking from an unstructured and apparently 'chaotic' realm into an established and regulated culture? Such concerns lie at the heart of this section and indeed at the heart of the feminist political vision. Many women believe that to understand them we must look very deeply at the foundations upon which our culture has been raised.

A rarely examined cornerstone of our thought is the idea that order is good and chaos is bad. We can see this ideology establishing itself in many ancient myths in which the process of creation is pictured as a struggle. Chaos, which is the fruitful source of potential from which life springs, is often pictured as female and dangerous. She must be tamed by the male forces of authority, law and regulation and in this process light is separated from darkness, life from death and good from evil. Traces of such thinking are clearly visible in the Hebrew scriptures.

We know, from historical study, that the societies which produced these myths were experiencing a very painful transition away from dependence upon the untamed natural environment, through the development of primitive technology, city life and more sophisticated civic structures based upon male dominance. Accompanying this transition was the development of new religious practices centred upon a male ruler. The disturbing but fruitful forces of 'chaos' were gradually banished from religious veneration although their disruptive power continued to be greatly feared.

The system beginning to be established, which feminists have loosely termed patriarchy, thus entailed not only the institutional power of men over women but also a related set of ideological motifs in which the principles of stability, order and 'civilization' are revered and the forces which challenge them are demonized and degraded. In which the voice of man becomes the voice of culture and the voice of woman a chaotic and incomprehensible tongue.

Although our modern civilization would find the tales and legends of ancient times obscure, the 'patriarchal system' under which we still live shares many of their basic assumptions. Christian cultures were built on the foundations of belief in a God who brought order out of chaos and who is all light, 'in Him is no darkness at all'. Furthermore, the political ideals which Christendom nurtured have encouraged us to strive for a civic system in which everything is harmonious and regulated. The utopian visions that inspire much social reform often contain the unconscious trace of yearning for a creation in which all the kinks have been ironed out; a future state of ordered perfection.

So all-pervasive has such thinking been that at first it appears difficult to challenge. Do we not all yearn for truth and goodness to triumph? However, feminists, amongst others, have lately called for a re-examination of such ideas perceiving them to contain dangerous assumptions about what must be silenced if such a harmony is to prevail. A culture which divides reality into two opposing realms of order and chaos and causes one to be worshipped and the other to be feared appears to be one which readily divides people along the same lines. Instead of realizing that we are immeasurably enriched by the voice of the outsider, the innovator, the stranger and those whose vulnerability or alternative perceptions of value challenge our own security we are quick to condemn and reject. A society in which racism, homophobia and sexism are enshrined from the height of institutional power to the level of nursery rhyme and children's games should give us pause to think long and hard about the soundness of its basic belief systems.

Whilst the history of feminism contains many examples of utopian thinking and feminists themselves have often spoken of the need for peace and harmony, there has always been an important perspective within women's politics that has been suspicious of the cruel voice of idealism which has marked both right and left wing political movements. At this particular point in time a dual emphasis appears to be emerging in feminist politics.

On the one hand feminists celebrate the vision for change that women have forged from their experience of marginality. Excluded from centres of power and influence and often experiencing poverty and insecurity, they have an insight into human history from the underside which is a revolutionary position from which to speak. It should lead us to examine our own creative potential as 'outsiders' and the strong links which bind us to those who have been similarly silenced.

The second emphasis is on the desire to articulate a political vision that does not have at its foundation the binary oppositions that so characterize patriarchy: binary oppositions that contrast the human and the divine, the spiritual and the physical, the chaotic present and the perfected future. These are opposites which divide us within ourselves as well as alienating us from each other.

Women are anxious that in picturing change we start from where we are, recognizing the strength that has been forged in suffering and admitting that many of the problems human beings encounter have no easy solutions. Certainly the better future we long for is not to be achieved by cutting off and condemning all that we fear but rather by looking with confidence at the realities of our situation and shaping these creatively into new forms and patterns.

Liberation theology has encouraged us to cherish a vision of a God who works from the underside of history weaving together what is cast aside and discarded into a fruitful and life generating resource. Similarly the central symbol of the Christian faith, the cross, is one to which many women turn when they want to describe the intractable pain of the creative process, the stubborn persistence of suffering at the heart of redemption and their realistic assessment of the cost that must be borne by those who offer their energies for the work of social transformation.

The sermons which have been brought together in this section all call for a re-evaluation of that which has been silenced and marginalized. They focus in varying ways upon what has been labelled as wild, wayward or lost according to dominant values and the ways in which these 'forces of chaos' might bring to birth new life both in the personal and social realms.

Susan Durber's Ash Wednesday sermon and the sermon entitled 'My Name is Carol' call for this process to begin at a deeply individual level with a re-assessment of our identities. We have been encouraged to despise and reject many of the forces that shape our humanity and for healing to occur these must be acknowledged and given their proper place. Janet Morley, Helen Stanton and Elizabeth Stuart celebrate the solidarity of the silenced ones and interpret this as a powerful redemptive force speaking from the edge with the power of Christ, the stranger and outsider. Jan Berry and Heather Walton ponder what political visions can sustain women's actions in barren times. They register that the conditions under which women act are not of their own choosing but might nevertheless nurture unseen potential in the same way as exile and exodus are inextricably linked in Hebrew thought. Finally, Angela Tilby's powerful Good Friday sermon reminds us that there is no place of refuge from the dark forces in creation but that the cross which draws together our light and our darkness is also the tree of life, 'laden with fruit and always green'.

ASH WEDNESDAY

Genesis 3.14–19; Psalm 8; Mark 1.9–14

A young sailor, little more than a boy, has committed some misdemeanour, some breaking of one of the many rules that keep the Navy what it is and what it ever shall be. The officer in charge devises his punishments to please his own sense of humour. Sometimes boys like this one are made to dig the garden with a fork – a table fork. In this case, the boy climbs into a dustbin in a corner of the parade ground. The other young sailors continue their drill and whenever the officer (a petty officer I suppose) comes by, he lifts the lid and bellows 'What are you boy?' The question is not a real one. The boy replies as he is bidden, 'I'm rubbish, Sir'. This goes on for some time, enough time for the boy to learn who he is. 'I'm rubbish.' You may think that barbaric – but I know it to have happened in this country in the early sixties in the Naval base where I spent my toddler years and where I began to learn who I am.

The preacher climbs into the pulpit and the congregation settle themselves into their chairs, confident that from this preacher they will indeed hear great wisdom and insight into the gospel of Jesus Christ. The preacher makes them wait, fingering his notes and positioning his spectacles precisely on his nose. He begins to speak. 'We are all shit', he says. The people gasp, not with horror, but with admiration. This preacher is well known for his insight into the human condition, for the width of his theological knowledge and for his low opinion of charismatic renewal. He prides himself on his Calvinist roots and for fun he reads Camus and Kierkegaard. The congregation nod at his words. They are not shocked by his strong language. Rather, they applaud his daring to name the human condition so well, in such 'contemporary' terms. 'Yes' they say to themselves, 'We are all shit'. They sit back now, waiting to hear that God, in his infinite goodness, loves them despite what they are. The lower and more disgusting their view of themselves, the more marvellous does the forgiving love of God seem. This preacher will certainly be asked again. You may think this story surprising, exaggerated or unbelievable, but I know it to be true. It happened in the college where I spent my undergraduate years and where I trained for the ministry, and where I continued to learn who I am.

I could tell other stories of how I learned who I am and who you are, but particularly who I am. Many of them could not properly be told here. Some would be stories common to many of us, some would be stories peculiar to me. I expect some of you have read the sermon about Hell in Joyce's *Portrait of the Artist* and felt yourselves to be little more than food for worms. Many of you experience the monthly shame which we are bidden to call a curse and to speak of only in whispers. Many of you will have strong and fleshly passions which have led you to shame and self loathing. Many of us have learnt that we are rubbish, that we are dirt and shame and death – and that we are to be grateful to God for loving us despite ourselves – being weak and foolish and loathesome. I have listened to sermons on the sin of pride and have tried ceaselessly to lower my opinion of myself. I have, at the minister's bidding, told God and told my brothers and sisters of my sin, of the rubbish in my soul. I have circumcised my life and shown a heart grief-rent. I have learnt who I am and who you are. Like the silly young sailor in the dustbin, I have cried out 'I'm rubbish'.

But, I have discovered that this is not the truth – this is a lie. I have discovered the lie, but still it has not quite relinquished its power. Maybe, for you there are other lies which snare you, other

falsehoods which grasp your heart. But don't let it be this one.
Don't believe the cruel voices that call you rubbish or worse.

I have heard the gospel in some strange places and with some
unexpected voices. In an Oxford lecture room with elegant
fireplace and latticed windows stands an Orthodox priest lectur-
ing on early Christian thought – the Fathers as he would put it. He
has arrived late and explains with a wry and knowing look that he
is late because someone stopped him on the way and asked for
his opinion on the ordination of women. He speaks, in sexist
language of course, about the nature of humankind. He is, as
ever, ready with an anecdote, a witticism, an aside. Today he says
that we are all like a man who has a raincoat. The coat has two
pockets and in each pocket there is a piece of paper. On one piece
of paper is written 'You are dust, and to dust you shall return'. On
the other is written 'You have made them a little lower than the
angels, crowned with glory and honour'. If one piece of paper is
lost, then the man is lost. If he holds both, then he lives. For one of
the very few women seated amongst the men in that Oxford
room, the sovereignty of God was indeed at hand. I repent.
I believe. I am not rubbish, I am a little lower than the angels –
even only a little lower than God. I am dust; I am earth, I can give
life and seed all the wonders of human life. And I am a little lower
than God. And so are all of you; not rubbish, not that other thing,
but dust and angel.

A rapid flick through the TV channels with the remote control
button produces a montage of our times; a flickering frieze of the
contemporary world with its disembodied images and apparently
meaningless frames. From this pastiche emerges one image; a
woman saying, 'They say we're scum round here, but I'm no
scum'. In front of a corporation brick wall, she lifts her hands in
protest and her voice is hard-edged. 'I'm, no scum'. Amen, amen.
I am no scum. I am dust, an earth creature, fashioned from the
rich, fertile soil of God's creating. And I am only a little lower
than the angels. I believe now that angels live in the vast urban
estates of our land, in the leaf-green suburbs and in the hills and
moorland. Noble creatures of dust reach with the tips of their
wings for the very nature of God. And all God's people shout
aloud to each other and to the great God who made them 'We are
no scum'.

Then there's a poem by Betjeman, an amusing silly man used to carrying his teddy bear about, who yet has seized the gospel. 'In a Bath Teashop':

'Let us not speak, for the love we bear one another –
Let us hold hands and look.'
She, such a very ordinary little woman;
He, such a thumping crook;
But both, for a moment, little lower than the angels
In the teashop's ingle-nook.[1]

Thumping crooks some of us are – there's no doubting that. There are people in the world who can steal a baby in its pram and throw the baby on to a rubbish heap, because they only wanted the pram. I have no illusions about the depths to which human beings may go. I know just how much lower than the angels some people can be. Now and again, I have come across people whom I might, given the courage, want to call scum in my rage and perplexity at what they have done. I do want to say that evil stretches its tentacles round the very roots of our being: that we need a saviour, a God to come and cross out evil's power. But I want more than anything to say that we are, all of us, only a little lower than the angels, even only a little lower than God. Of utter depravity I can no longer speak. I see too well the power of those words to crush the human spirit and to drain life where it might surge passionate and strong. God names us as earth creatures, children of the dust, but not of ashes, not of the rubbish heap, no scum. God names us as angels, almost gods, not demons or devils. You are dust and to dust you shall return – and – you are a little lower than God.

I have, some of you will say, forsaken the faith of my fathers. I refuse to hear now that old chestnut that original sin is the only doctrine you can prove empirically. I am tired of hearing that a kind of pseudo-Calvinist pessimism about human nature is the only alternative to a silly, naive and empty optimism. I am weary of a God who loves me only in spite of my dirtiness and sin, a God who wants to save me from a mire that I begin to doubt is really there. I am sick of thinking myself and my sisters (and brothers) rubbish and, the other thing. I want to accuse my fathers of claiming power over me by crushing my soul and the souls of others, by plying us with sackcloth and ashes when our hearts long to sing in the cool clean air and our feet want to dance on the rich earth. Now I am unafraid of their labels; whether Pelagian or (mysteriously) Semi-Pelagian, whether they think me naive or sentimental, heretic, rebel or witch. I know now what I am. I am dust. And I am a little lower than god. Call me what you like. And let them call you what they like. You are dust, earth creatures. And you are a little lower than gods.

I love the story of Jesus wandering in the wilderness. I love it because it is a story of Jesus with us. There in the bleak dust land of the wilderness, Jesus walked for forty days. He was with the wild beasts, with the creatures of the earth. And he was there with the angels, with the creatures of heaven. And he was tempted by Satan. In this montage of earth and angel and tempting Satan we find ourselves. We are earth creature and angel winged. Evil assails us, but is not with us. The wild beasts of earth are with us and angels wait for us to be like them, but evil is not with us. In Jesus we see one who was fully human, at home with the earth and with the angels. Through this human life God finds us and proclaims the end of all that would name us as evil. Born on to the pressed-down dust floor of a stable, Jesus, who was not even a little lower than God, tells us we are not our own. We belong to the nature of God and to the nature of the earth. And evil and death shall have no dominion.

We are dust, you and I. We are dust, always returning to the rich nobility of earth. And we are a little lower than god, you and I, always returning to the true and beautiful source of our being. The time is fulfilled; repent and believe in the good news.

[1] John Betjeman, 'In a Bath Tea Shop', *Collected Poems*, John Murray (Publishers) Ltd.

Susan Durber

MY STORY, MY SONG

My name is Carol. I am a woman, I am a Christian, I am a feminist. Or maybe I should say I am becoming a woman, becoming a Christian, becoming a feminist. Because being all those is a process – a process of becoming. I am still becoming what I am, still being born. The labour has been long. The labour has been painful. The labour has been worth it.

So, what do I believe? what do I stand for? What are the guidelines by which I live my life? What is my creed as a Christian, and a feminist, and a woman? I believe that I am a person of power. I believe that I am free to choose how I live my life, to make my own decisions, to take control of my own future. I believe I must take responsibility for the mistakes I make, and take credit for the good and generous actions I perform. I believe that I have the right to stand upright before God. And I believe that whatever I do, I will always be loved, because God never stops loving. I believe that while my story is my own, it overlaps with the stories of all women, everywhere.

What am I? Who do I say that I am? I am a proclaimer of the gospel – of crucifixion and of resurrection. And I am a person of gifts: gifts given to me by my fellow-travellers and by God, and gifts which *I* have to give to others and to God. My model is the Christ, the poured-out Christ, ever-renewed. These are my beliefs. This is what I stand for. These are my guidelines for living my life. This is who I am. Spelled out in these proud words.

But it was not always like this. I was not always strong. I did not always have power. I have not always had a self to pour out. This is my story. My labour of giving birth to myself began when I named myself a victim, when I began the process of remembering, and at the same time entered the most painful and the most freeing period of my life. I am not lacking in courage. And this took every particle of courage I had. And sometimes it seemed as if even that would not be enough and I would be broken in pieces by the weight of what I discovered. And once I began, I discovered things fast.

Perhaps it may seem strange that the words 'You have been very severely abused' should have been words of comfort and relief. But they were uttered by my therapist – the first person who ever took seriously the pain I had always carried with me. What I had not realized, and what many people still do not realize, is that emotional abuse of children can be just as devastating as sexual abuse and produces many of the same effects. Although the physical violation was not so blatantly present, it was still there in my life – as was the violation of my mind and my spirit – violations which occurred over and over again over a long period of time and were thus deeply insidious. It took me a long while to see myself as a victim worthy of the same kinds of help and healing which are offered to victims of sexual and violent physical abuse. I was well trained in the belief that denigration, and belittling, and the slow destruction of creativity and joy were appropriate for little girls.

It is perhaps difficult for those who have not experienced prolonged emotional abuse to understand how a series of apparently small incidents can contribute towards breaking a child so completely that she carries a wound into adulthood – a wound so deep that it prevents her functioning as a whole human being, either emotionally, physically, or mentally. Most of the things which I suffered are done to some degree by most parents, even the most loving. Some of the most damaging occurrences in my childhood are very like behaviour I have heard described as 'good Christian parenting'. Perhaps that is why so little attention is paid to the effects of emotional abuse on children, or the ways in which they might be healed. It is actually quite threatening to face the possibility that someone like you might be an abuser. It was not so much *what* was done to me in my childhood which did the damage – although some traumatic incidents did occur – it was the cumulative effect over many years of a series of humiliations, rejections, ridiculings, and accusations of selfishness, defiance, stupidity, guile, and deceit. A child may get over being told once that 'Mummy cannot love you when you are naughty'. A child cannot get over being told that over and over again and never being told about Mother's love in any other context. (What price calling God 'Mother' now?)

If that were all, maybe the wounding would not have gone so deep, but there is much, much more. You do not need to know all the small woundings which finally became a damaging that was almost too much for me to bear. All you need to know is enough to convince you that it is not necessary to rape a child or beat her nearly to death to go a great way towards destroying her. It can be done slowly and gradually. And it too often is. My story is not an isolated one. I am not alone.

I said that I preach crucifixion *and* resurrection, and I do. For me, the crucifixion image will always be a deeply significant one. But it is not an image of powerlessness. Because now I *choose* to take as my model the Christ whose self was poured out – the Christ who himself chose to be poured out. And this is a choice for me because I am no longer empty as I once was. I am no longer sucked dry of feeling and love and warmth. I have been filled – by God and by others. And I have a self to pour out. I can make a choice to do it. I have discovered that I am actually quite a generous person by nature. The choice is a natural one for me. I am not *and never was* the selfish, demanding child of my mother's warped imagining. And my image of crucifixion is enriched by my experience of resurrection. I have risen and I will continue to be raised. And only because I am constantly being raised am I able to begin to imitate the poured-out Christ. This is my gospel, and my journey, my birthing, has empowered me to formulate it and begin to live it out.

This is my gospel. And I say 'my' gospel because I would not presume to prescribe it for others. It is a gospel which I only learned after I had begun to discard all the confining, constricting cords which bound me throughout my childhood and on into adulthood. *All* the cords, including the religious ones. For my childhood was a 'religious' one. My mother would tell you that she has always believed in God. And so she has. And so have I. As a child, I believed that God loved all people and especially children. I believed that if you asked for forgiveness, the evil and wicked things you had done would be wiped out and you would be 'washed as white as snow'. I believed that God gave great gifts. I believed that Jesus rose from the dead. I believed all those things. If you had asked me what I believed, I would have told you all those things, and I would have told you in all sincerity.

I believed them, but I had rarely experienced them. Somehow, it never occurred to me that the rare, warm, sun-filled moments of my life were an almost permanent state of affairs for some people – for other children, for loved children. One of the most powerful moments in my therapy was when I discovered why I had always felt different from most of the other children I knew. Loved children *were* different from me. Not only had I not experienced being bathed in love, being secure, feeling safe, feeling clean, being given gifts for which there was no price to be paid, I did not know how to experience all those things. But I have begun to learn. And it has not been easy. The old patterns of defence which had served me so well, which had helped me to survive, had to be unlearned so that I would be able to trust myself and others in the future. My suspicion of being offered 'gifts' had to be overcome, so I could learn to receive from those who loved me, and from God. My defences against the 'weakness' of weeping had to be broken down so I could grieve properly. I had been broken so many times, and now I was choosing to contribute to my own breaking so I could begin to grow – and grow healthily, and proudly, and truly.

Somehow, the church seems to expect that people will 'naturally' know how to feel the love God has for them, how to recognize what it feels like to be forgiven, how to bring about and experience resurrection in their lives. Somehow the church expects people to know what it means to feel confident that they are made in the image of God and are power-filled human beings. And maybe it is true that if our lives are lived out as God intended us to live them, those feelings and experiences *do* come 'naturally'. But they do not to all people. It is as if the abuse of children builds some kind of a wall between those children and the possibility of a natural, instinctive good relationship with God. Telling a person who has never felt unconditional love that this is what God's love is like is meaningless. Telling a person whose smallest childhood misdemeanours were rarely forgiven and even more rarely forgotten that God forgives people's sins and 'wipes them out' is just a form of words.

The church should not be telling abused women and men what they ought to be feeling, but enabling them to feel it. It should not be telling them what God's love is like, but accepting them as they are – just as God does. Not trying to teach them what the Bible says about Crucifixion, Exodus, and Exile, but listening to what *they* have to tell about rejection, alienation, and slow death. For it is not all one way. I am not asking the Body of Christ to bring me wholeness, give me healing, and affirm me, while I offer nothing in return. I am no longer the little girl who could give nothing because she had so little to give and that little she needed to survive. For I, too, have gifts to give. I have experiences to offer.

I have *my* experiences to offer – *my* story, *my* song. The Exodus, the Exile, the Valley of the Shadow, and the Passion. All these – and true resurrection.

Carol

'DESIRE FOR OTHER THINGS'*

Isaiah 5.1–7; Mark 4.3–20

> And others are the ones sown among unproductive weeds; they are those who hear the word, but the preoccupations of the present age, and the seductiveness of wealth, and the desire for other things, enter in and crowd out the word, and it becomes unfruitful. (Mark 4.18–19)

'The desire for other things' – I have for some time felt that a good many of the problems we face in our world are problems of desire. I don't mean the desires we know about and have problems with: desires we feel ashamed of and try to erase because we fear they are sinful; desires we feel pain about because they are unfulfilled; or desires which we have consciously acted on but which turned out to have problematic consequences we had not foreseen. I don't mean any of those. I mean the problem of not knowing what it is that we really desire. Choosing what to give our life to. Knowing what kind of world we want. Let's face it, most of us have, or will have, many possible choices for our lives. We can get choked with choice, as the word of God in this parable is described as getting choked, crowded out, by all the 'other things' which we don't exactly choose but which grow anyway, like virulent weeds which, particularly at this time of year, appear from nowhere, are at first hard to distinguish from the seedlings you've planted, but in fact grow faster and block their sunlight.

---

* A sermon given at Magdalen College Oxford for Christian Aid Week, May 1992.

Now, whether this explanation that follows the well-known parable of the sower is from the lips of Jesus, or reveals the mind of the early church as it reflected on its own problems, it highlights this crucial point. How we react to the word of God depends on where we are – what kind of ground we're standing on. And our ground is already a bit crowded. The last time I heard the parable read and expounded in a service the context couldn't have been more different. It was a few of us around a ramshackle table in the dusk out of doors in a remote village in the Philippines, where I was travelling with Christian Aid. The eucharist was celebrated with lemon biscuits and water, because that's all there was. After the reading of the Gospel everyone who wanted to had a chance to speak. Now those Filipino peasants, because of the dusty ground they were standing on, did not have a problem identifying their desires, knowing what they passionately wanted. They want clean water, so that they can drink without getting ill. They want basic health care, so that they don't have to watch their children die of preventable diseases like TB and diarrhoea. They want access to land, to grow their own food – in fact they want to go back home, to the houses and fields they have been evicted from by their own government's military. They want to live without fear of violence. And they are quite certain God wants those things for them too. I found, in that place, a rather unnerving but also exhilarating clarity which I've never found at home. The word and promise of God is heard very sharply there – it's sort of naked and obvious. You can't miss it.

What are the things that cloak the sharpness of God's word for us? The parable speaks of 'the preoccupations of the present age'. The translations tend to speak misleadingly of the 'cares of this world', as if the problem were just the ordinary multiplicity of tasks and responsibilities and anxieties that everyone faces in an individual life. Actually I think it refers to what our world cares about. What are the ideologies that our society in fact surrounds us with, makes us feel to be normal or unchangeable, gets us to spend our lives serving, without really noticing them? In a place like Oxford, it's deceptively easy to believe we are not unawarely subject to such pressures, simply because we are trained to recognize and analyse and criticize theories in a systematic way. The problem is, we are not on the whole asked to choose a theory and actually live by it. So we can become highly articulate over dinner about all sorts of things, including the causes of world poverty, and still live lives whose actual choices – what we eat, where we live, who we live with, what work we do, where we educate our children – are governed by quite other criteria, just like everyone else.

And what about 'the seductiveness of wealth'? You may well feel, as you struggle to make ends meet on a derisory grant and quite possibly mounting debts, that you are not in danger of being distracted by 'delight in riches'. But the heart of seduction is not irresistible desire, it's about finding yourself entangled in a situation you don't remember choosing. You didn't notice the moment when you should or could have said no, but you're now in the power of something stronger than you and you're deeply compromised and committed. We have not been helped by the tradition of preaching about the power of money as if all that's required is a little easy detachment – a little tasteful moderation in our pleasure at owning things. The problem about money is the way it sets the terms before you've thought about them. What is more likely to commit you to serving the rules of the financial markets of our world than to find yourself in long-term debt, good and early? This kind of entanglement is exactly where the Third World finds itself in relation to the governments and banks of the West. For us, how to pay our debts and mortgages shapes our individual lives (and our political affiliations). For the poorest people in our world, it's a matter of life and death.

So how do we get to hear clearly the word of God, how do we find out what we really desire, how do we see the connections between those two things? Well, one way, curiously, is to notice what it is we find revolting. If we turn to the Old Testament reading, we find it is all about desire, about longing, and about being revolted. The passage begins – 'Let me sing for my beloved a love song concerning his vineyard.' A love-song about a vineyard? Odd. Although keen gardeners do know about real grief when beloved and costly plants die. I've only recently got into plants and my teenage children clearly see it as a symptom of my advanced senility – or at least of the pathetic boredom of my life compared with the wild passions of theirs. Don't you believe it. There is something very primal about getting your hands in the soil, touching roots, watching that fierce and lush new growth push through. Anyway, the vineyard owner waits passionately for the harvest which should come from the choicest vines he has planted. And what does he get? Again, English translations tend to be less than gutsy in conveying the sense here. They talk coyly about 'wild grapes' or 'sour fruit'. But in fact the word means 'stinking things'. Something not just to be angry about, but revolted by. I'm not sure what the writer could have meant in relation to grapes. Perhaps it was some loathsome fungal disease – hence the smell – which explains why the hedges had to be destroyed and the infected soil left fallow. The punchline of this terse poem hammers home what it is that God is revolted by – namely what is going on in the prophet's own immediate culture:

> The vineyard of the Lord of hosts is the house of Israel
> and the people of Judah are his pleasant planting;
> and he looked for justice, but behold, bloodshed;
> for righteousness, but behold, a cry!

There are some startling bits of wordplay in the Hebrew here. The word for justice מִשְׁפָּט (*mishpat*) is very like the word for blood-shed מִשְׂפָּח (*mispach*) and the word for righteousness, צְדָקָה (*zᵉdākāh*) with hardly a change, becomes a cry of anguish צְעָקָה (*zᵉʿākāh*). It is as if the people addressed have sort of misheard the word of God, and God's requirement, and have achieved blood-shed, thinking that sounds near enough to justice. Or perhaps the similarity of the words seems to justify an inability on the people's part to notice the stink of what is not only an inadequate response, it's revolting. Either way, the irony is searing.

But looking at the world, it's clear that on the whole we don't find injustice, violence, innocent suffering anything like revolting enough. We seem to find it tolerable, necessary, ordinary, the way things are. Perhaps we are not well-placed to notice what it is that smells suspect.

To go back to that Filipino village, where certain things were clear. After the eucharist that night, they told me the story of how they had been evicted from their homes by soldiers. In their fear and panic, there hadn't been time to round up the animals – mainly pigs and chickens which are crucial to their meagre income – but everything had been abandoned as the forest was cleared and turned into a no-man's land because the soldiers believed rebels were active there. Later, four of the bravest villagers decided to go back to try and rescue the animals. They never returned. Their friends were scared to go into the forest to look for them, but they gradually widened their search. One day someone followed the sound of buzzing flies and found the bodies of their friends rotting there. The authorities were informed, but nothing was ever done. Instead, the villagers were given some black plastic bags and disinfectant and told to get on with burying the bodies themselves.

One cannot miss the fact that this is a revolting story. It is also not an isolated one in the Third World. Unrest, eviction from land, violent military repression focussed on the poorest lack of redress harassment of those who try to improve things for the poor – all these are common. Some of you may have seen that programme in the 'One World' series which showed the officially connived-at liquidation of street kids in Brazil. What is not always clear to us is the revolting nature of the connections between the society we live in and those acts of bloodshed, those cries of distress. One of the main connections is the external debt that these countries are effectively enslaved to. Unrest exists in the Philippines because eighty per cent of people are desperately poor and getting poorer. They are getting poorer because in order to pay the interest on its massive debt the government has, on the instructions of the International Monetary Fund, removed subsidies on basic foodstuffs like rice, cut already inadequate spending on basic health care and education, and in short done whatever it can to sell off its forests and the best of its land to foreign companies that pay in dollars.

The stories behind the contracting of many of these debts give off bad smells when you take the lid off. Back in the seventies the Western banks were keen to lend money, and decided it was safe to lend to shaky or tyrannical Third World regimes, so long as the government underwrote it, because a country couldn't go bankrupt, could it? They were often irresponsible in making investments. One classic example is the Bataan Nuclear Power plant. Western companies and banks, including, at that time, one of our high street banks were involved. Quite apart from the allegations of bribery and corruption that have been against the process of allocating the contract to the builders, it was discovered that the plant is sited on a earthquake zone and it will never be safe enough to function. But the Filipino people will probably never be able to stop paying for it. In recent years the Freedom from Debt Coalition there has researched the circumstances of many of the loans, and has called for those debts which were contracted corruptly to be repudiated. This was one of them. But the financial markets have overtaken them. In order to win a necessary rescheduling of the timetable of some repayments, the Philippines government has been obliged to sign a deal which included agreeing that this debt was legitimate, before it could be tested in the courts. So the cost will go on being paid by the poor. I think this story stinks just as much as the other one. It is in this context that the Episcopal Church in the Philippines, a sister church to our own Anglican Church here, has called for the total repudiation by its government of the external debt, referring to it as the 'shadow of death' which hovers upon every home. And, significantly, it promises the government that 'we will stand by you in any dark alleys that we may all enter as a consequence of reprisals that may come as a result'. I think the document has chosen its metaphors with great accuracy.

So I think that the capacity to feel revolted, including about things to do with global systems that present themselves as neutral and bound by laws we can't change, is a good and indeed godly sign. It's a gut feeling, it's strong, it's alive. It makes you know for sure that things are not how they are meant to be. It makes you know for sure what kind of a world you really want and desire. And that you aren't going to tolerate what shouldn't be tolerated. Interestingly, it isn't the same as feeling despairing, or depressed, or powerless. It has a lot of energy behind it, energy that is full of passion, energy to choose change. The Christian Aid Week theme is 'We believe in life before death' – and I think that passionate desire, and passionate revulsion, are both part of our longing for life itself, our refusal to surrender to the forces of death.

I know this, because the people of that Filipino village know it even more fiercely than I do. They shared with me their outrage and their pain – but also their hope, determination and faith.

Next morning, Mulon and Rosalinda and others woke me up early and we went back to their old village from which they had been evacuated – on the way I saw some of their stilted wooden houses gradually falling down in disrepair. In front of the empty chapel they showed me a grave with a simple wooden cross. At its foot were flowers in a jam jar and some candles. The heat of the sun had withered the flowers and the candles had melted and sort of sprawled all down the side of the jam jars. It was very basic and ordinary. Yet, in that early morning, it felt a bit like being taken to visit the resurrection tomb. Here they had buried in a place of honour their brave friends who were killed, and I knew that the candles and flowers would constantly be renewed. For the placing of that grave is a sign that one day they will all go back. They will pray in that chapel, they will work those fields, they will rebuild those houses. They will never lose their God-given sense of being revolted by injustice, of longing for what is right. They will not accept a world which produces the 'stinking things' of injustice and bloodshed – and nor should we. But they look for the harvest of God's word, which, in the teeth of the evidence, will produce thirty fold, sixty fold, one hundred fold.

Janet Morley

CANDLEMAS HOMILY

In the Christian year Candlemas is a pivotal time, the time when the shadow of the cross begins to fall upon the joy of Christmas. It is the time when the story of the appalling massacre of innocents begins to reveal itself as a prefiguring of the death of Jesus.

For Mary the offering of her child is a time of fulfilment, but also of foreboding. The one whom she has brought to birth is revealed as one set for the rise and fall of many in Israel, is a sign that is destined to be opposed. The price of Mary's yes to God appears to be more costly still. For a sword will pierce your own soul also.

What God is bringing to birth in us is also immensely costly. It may already have required appalling changes – not only for ourselves, but for our families and friends. For some of us there may have been excruciating and continuing pain. For God asks us to push away our comfortable naiveté, to face the sorrow of the world, its grinding poverty, its violence, its anguish. Deep within ourselves there may have been the frightening risk of losing the very self with whom we have been familiar. Maybe our ingrained niceness is opened up to a whole range of feelings which threaten chaos and irrationality and lack of control. The grace which brings that of God to birth within us *is* endless gift, but it can cost us not less than everything.

In El Salvador I met Marta, a woman, a Franciscan novice, in her mid thirties, full of energy and passion when she spoke, but without hatred. I spent a few days at her convent, and one evening we sat in the courtyard, overlooked as always by an artillery post, and she told me something of her history. She had been born, not among the richest in the land, but among those who were rich enough, and educated, but not challenging of the status quo. Her family had sent her to university in the United States, and while there she had begun to sense a glimmering of a vocation to the religious life. Her family, like most, rich and poor, in El Salvador were devout Catholics, and saw this as an intelligible and honourable possibility. Marta's sojourn in the States however, had brought with it a critical awareness of what was happening in her own country. In exploring her vocation this meant the way was by no means obvious. Her family wondered about a contemplative order, but decided a teaching order, educating the daughters of the rich, more suited to her temperament.

Marta took her time, she even spent two years with one of the teaching orders, but she left and became a Franciscan, living in a barracks town, working in a parish made up of seventy, mostly rural communities, some of which were across the river in territory controlled by the left wing guerrilla group, the FMLN. She went to be alongside the poor and as far as she could to share their lives, and so their suffering. Later, when she made her first profession, she made a vow, alongside the traditional vows, to accompany the poor and oppressed.

The gift of vocation which brought with it immense joy for Marta was to be costly, and to go on being costly. Alienation from her family, surges of anger and hatred against the powerful which undermined her self image and her sense of God's love, the inconveniences of living the life of the poor, and its dangers, all became a part of her experience. It was eternal life for her, as I saw in the light in her eyes, and her clenched fist as she spoke of the struggles of the poor. She did not hesitate in her love for them, but sometimes she wondered about the future and how her hope might be sustained in the face of such frequent violence. Like Mary she watched the ones she loved suffer and die. Yes, she shared the important small steps to liberation with rejoicing, indeed they were the stuff of life, but even those were at times overshadowed by a fear that the army would take away achievements like improvements in health care or growth in self esteem.

Candlemas reminds me that the gift which we have rejoiced in and cherished, and which has been for us a taste of eternal life, is also overshadowed by the cross. It is not a resting place, nor ours to cling to.

Many of us here, and I include myself, are experiencing times of transition. My own experience is of yet again having to let go familiar securities. It is a state, uncomfortable, yet energizing, of simply not knowing. It is a time of waiting, waiting expectantly, but waiting, none the less, for it is not in my control. Yet I may not be passive, for I must also nurture this new unknown thing, I must do the work which God has given me to do: work on myself, and the continuingly painful struggle of working for justice. I trust and believe that this has to do with a bringing to birth of new life in me, though it doesn't always feel like that.

Last year I visited for the first time the Corrymeela Community, the ecumenical community for peace and reconciliation in Northern Ireland. I rose early each day and stood on the cliff rejoicing in the amazing beauty of the coast of North Antrim. I was warmed by the sun, and by long prayerful silences before breakfast, in the chapel. I reflected upon my devotion to Mary and what it might mean. And, among many other activities, I went to Portadown. There I spent two hours with four Catholic women who are the heart of the faith and justice group in that community, and whose passionate working, and honesty and persistence moved me enormously.

In many ways they were very ordinary women, who had left

school at fourteen to work in the linen factories, who had married early and had children who were now in their teens and twenties. But they had asked questions, about inequalities between the two communities in Northern Ireland, about the loyalist march which passed through their town, about unemployment and the fears of their children They knew their own anger and hatred and asked themselves how all this made sense for them as Christian women.

They began to work ecumenically, and therefore riskily, visiting women's groups in the other community and finding an experience very like their own. They worked for years with groups of elderly people and eventually brought some of them together for an ecumenical Christmas party. They have protested about the route of the loyalist march, and the treatment of their children, convinced that they had the right to equity. Yet they do not know what will happen to their children or their country, nor what will result from their work for justice. They are astonishingly powerful women, who pray and work quietly, and long for peace, and trust that their work will help to bring reconciliation, though they do not see it.

Those four women, their faces and their voices and the swirl of their cigarette smoke, have entered into my prayers, and so as I come to Candlemas, to the gospel which so focusses upon Mary, they accompany me and illuminate my vision of her. Mary, who lifted up the voice of prophecy in the Magnificat now glimpses sorrow and suffering and pain. But in letting go her gift, her child, into the ways of God, she releases new life into the world. Amen.

Helen Stanton

DO NOT BE AFRAID*

I want to share with you some thoughts that have occupied me as I have been embroiled in the fight over my gay and lesbian prayer book, *Daring to Speak Love's Name*[1]. I have had to think a great deal about Jesus' command in the Sermon on the Mount:

---

* A sermon for Lesbian and Gay Pride given at Bloomsbury Baptist Church, London in June 1992

Love your enemies and pray for those who persecute you
(Matt.5.43).

And I think it is particularly appropriate as we celebrate our pride
in being who we are, that those of us who claim to follow the
person of Jesus of Nazareth meditate on this commandment. For
it is this commandment that separates us from all other gay and
lesbian people and indeed I suspect that large numbers of the gay
and lesbian community would regard our attempt to obey this
commandment as a sign of weakness on our part, a sign of our
lack of commitment to the 'cause', a sign of our collaboration
with the oppressors and so on. And, to be honest, those of us who
are Christian and believe ourselves to be completely committed to
the cause are often tempted to forget Jesus' words about our
enemies. It is easier to forget. It is easier to fight against people,
and the systems they stand for and perpetuate, if we demonize
them, if we no longer see them as people but as 'enemies'. And
how are we supposed to love people who hate and oppress us? To
answer that question we turn to the life of Jesus of Nazareth.

What can we learn about loving our enemies from the example
of Jesus? Well, first we can scotch the myth that loving your
enemies involves becoming 'soft', giving in to them and refraining
from challenging them. Jesus suffered and died for 'the cause' of
God's kingdom and he was executed by his enemies because he
refused to capitulate to them. I'm afraid loving your enemies does
not mean that you end up sharing a bottle of whisky in the golf
club with them. It does not immunize you from suffering. In fact,
loving your oppressors is likely to threaten them even more
because you are refusing to play their game and you are more
likely to end up on a cross than at the golf club on a Friday
afternoon.

So what does loving our enemies actually involve? I think that
Jesus teaches that loving people who are 'out to get you' involves
refusing to play by the rules of war. It involves refusing to
dehumanize people, to see them as the 'enemy'. It involves seeing
them at all times as God sees them, as people made in the image of
God, as people with emotions, fears and hopes like you and me. As
people who, like it or not, we are bound to in love and interdependence. This means that we have a duty to treat them with respect,

we have a duty to keep reaching out to them and talking to them. We cannot simply give up on them. If you read the Hebrew scriptures you cannot help but be struck by the way in which Yahweh (God) simply refuses to give up on the people. They keep rejecting God, God keeps being hurt but never has enough and says 'Sod this I'm off to find a new chosen people'. Yet God never goes soft on the people either, but keeps demanding justice, peace and righteousness from them. Similarly with Jesus, he never stops talking to those who are out to get him. He doesn't execute any of them. And when one reads the Gospels the reason why becomes obvious: there is always the chance that he will get through, that they will change – and some do.

It takes an awful lot of courage to keep relating to people who hate and despise you and want to destroy you. And this is why, if I were asked to define what it means to love your enemies, I would say 'To love your enemies is the refusal to be afraid of them'. We all know that it is fear that generates most homophobia, it is fear that stops most gay and lesbian people from coming out and it is fear that divides us one from another. If we can conquer fear, we can conquer hate. And this is what the gospel is about, the good news is that there is no need to be afraid anymore. Why? Because of the resurrection. The resurrection is God's promise to us that in the end death, hatred, injustice, and fear will not have the last word. In the end, love, life, justice and peace will triumph. The divine injunction 'Do not be afraid' chimes through the Gospels like a bell of victory, from the appearance of the angel to Zechariah, to the appearances of Jesus after the resurrection. I just wish that those of us who call ourselves Christians actually believed that! It makes me so angry when I see Christians acting if they were not saved, spending hours and hours indulging in so-called spiritual activities, which are really only a form of spiritual masturbation because they cannot believe they have been saved. We have been saved for a purpose and that is to free us from guilt and fear so that we can help in the building up of God's commonwealth on earth. Remember Jesus' words to Mary at the tomb 'Do not cling on to me'. I sometimes think that we spend too much time clinging on to Jesus and not enough time following him. It is comforting to cling on like a baby at its mother's breasts, much more frightening to be thrust out into the world and be told to change it. But that is what Jesus does. When he sends his disciples out the Greek word used is *ekballion* – literally pushed out!

We have no excuse to be afraid. As Christians we should not be on the margins of the gay and lesbian community or movement, we should be right at the centre. We should be taking on governments, systems, injustices, as our Saviour did. Because we love our enemies, we must take them on, challenge them and change them. We have to take the risk and the risk can lead to crucifixion but it can also lead to miracles, as I myself have witnessed. I have been through a horrible experience. When I decided to reveal to the media that SPCK was planning to drop my book and that the Archbishop of Canterbury had been dragged into the plot, I did not know whether I was saying goodbye to my career, family, privacy, safety and good name. I was terrified, but it was worth it because of the hundreds of people who aligned themselves with the lesbian and gay cause for the first time. A group of us had the courage to overcome the fear of taking on a major religious publishing house and the Archbishop of Canterbury. It was a frightening experience yet we overcame the injustice and the homophobia.

Many of you will know that during the height of the civil rights movement in the USA a new verse was added to the popular protest song 'We shall overcome'. The new verse goes like this 'We are not afraid, we are not afraid, we are not afraid, today …' That is the song of the angels, of Jesus, of the first apostles, martyrs and saints, it is the song of the oppressed throughout the world in all ages and it must be our song. It is a song to be sung in the presence of our enemies for it is saying, 'I love and respect you too much, I want you to change too much, for me to be afraid of you.' It is the song of those who believe in resurrection and therefore it must be our song during the celebration of who we are and in the fight for justice.

[1] In April 1992 SPCK, a major religious publishing house attached to the Church of England, decided to abandon the publication of a book of prayers, blessings and liturgies for lesbian and gay Christians. SPCK had commissioned the book and it had received excellent readers' reports. The Archbishop of Canterbury was involved in the internal discussion of the book as president of the society. Whilst making it clear that he did not want to interfere in the editorial policy of SPCK he could not support

publication of the book because of the society's links with the Church of England and he warned that he would have to consider his position as president if SPCK continued to publish books which he could not agree with. The book, *Daring to Speak Love's Name*, was later published by Hamish Hamilton.

Elizabeth Stuart

HEBREW WOMEN/EGYPTIAN WOMEN

God does not always grant life, fertility and growth – or at least, if we are to look at what experience teaches us, whilst growth luxuriates in some areas others are barren and bleak. Perhaps it would be best to picture God working with two hands. Whatever one touches burgeons into bud, blossom and fruit. Where the fingers of the other fall sap stops flowing, stems wither and harvests fail.

It is a bitter experience to feel your life restrained in this way. God has sealed the fountain, stopped the womb and hardened the heart. Despite our labouring in the field and the watering of our tears, no growth comes. Eventually the top soil blows away exposing the drying roots and so it seems that the sand below will now never support life. Not in another season, not in ten years time or in ten thousand.

Hard times, barren times. It is not surprising that those who feel their own vitality failing sometimes look with hatred on those whom God appears to have blessed with increase.

> The children of Israel were fruitful … they increased and grew immensely.
> The new king of Egypt grew frightened.
> 'We must take steps' he said 'to stop this growth'.

I longed for a child for many years and I did not conceive. A common experience for any woman to have in any time but one which for me came to symbolize many things about my experience in this country at this time. It felt as if my personal and bodily reality was but one aspect of a much wider drama. In fact it seemed hardly surprising that I could not conceive when death seemed to have touched so much around me. I felt as if the hand of God had fallen heavily, not just on me but on my culture, my class and generation. Vision, creativity and justice were withering away. I could still acknowledge life profligate and abundant elsewhere but I walked in shadow.

The experience was the more vivid because I live in the inner city. Light shines harshly in such places exposing many contrasts. I walk through the streets in fashionable clothes, carrying books in my rucksack and money in my pockets. Firm step, flat stomach, somewhere to go in life beyond the close packed rows of grimey houses. Other women look at me and their looks are those of tacit knowledge that we inhabit different worlds. I look back on them seeing their bondage to poverty, to the heavy demands of servicing men and children. I see the limits to their freedom and yet I envy them.

I do envy their swollen stomachs and the children that cling to breasts and knees of women aged fourteen to fifty. I envy the apparent ease and carelessness of their procreation and compare it to my own anxious child-fearing circles. But my envy is more than that of the ambiguous blessing of large numbers of babies.

I recognize the hand of God has brought life here. A strength to survive these harsh days when there is no straw given to mix with the clay. To these women pressed under a harsh regime has been given something I lack. It is a power difficult to name without sentimentality and yet what they possess defies romance and sentiment. It is knowledgeable and resilient. Their children drink in this strength with their mothers' milk. It grants them some immunity to the hopelessness that I feel when I survey our common streets. When I give up they will carry on. They are stronger than I am. They know this and I know it too.

Reflecting upon the poignant experience of infertility whilst living in a part of town which has a massively higher than average number of children has been my particular experience. However, I know that I am not alone in my longing to share in the creation of new life and in yearning for changes in the way we live now. Many white, middle class women like me have given long hours of work and invested something of their very selves in the movements and campaigns that have been part of our efforts to stem the political tide that flows against us. I know that the sense of despair I have felt as precious things have been destroyed is their sense also. We stand in shadow unable to protect those things we cherish and unable to conceive new things to take their place.

But, just as I am moved to acknowledge the procreative strength that God has given to the women who I pass each day on the streets, so my friends and I can raise our heads from our collective despair at the success of our own efforts – we are able to point a finger and say, 'I see life there'. White middle class women wistfully celebrate the vitality of working class women, the black women's movement and the defiant strength of women triumphing against their oppressors in other parts of the world. But how should we who feel our own strength ebbing relate to our sisters to whom God has granted life?

> The Hebrew women were strong despite their hard labour with clay and bricks and in the fields. God granted them increase and many children were born to them, so many that the Egyptians feared them.

As I think about those of us who feel the order to which we belong is dying and deserves to die, I wonder, did all their neighbours fear the Hebrews? Certainly the king and the rulers of the land appeared to sense their coming downfall in the flourishing of their slaves. Perhaps most of the Egyptians shared this premonition and fear made them even more vicious in their oppression. But maybe there were others conscious of the rottenness on which their civilization stood? Perhaps some women saw similarities between their own position and those of the Hebrews in bondage? I am sure yet others were simply moved by compassion at the suffering they witnessed daily and began to harbour a sense of admiration at the strength of their victims.

> Pharaoh's daughter came down to the river to bathe. She and the women who attended her walked along the riverside and saw a basket with a baby in it hidden in the reeds. The child was crying and she felt pity for it.

It is not wrong to perceive the hand of God at work in others and, when you stand in shadow, to testify the light still shines elsewhere. However, if you are barren yourself it is very tempting to try and become the mother of another's child. When you feel your own efforts are wasted and yet life is springing up from another's labour the desire is there to take something of their abundant harvest for your own. This is what I and many women like me have often fallen into the trap of doing. We seize the life that God has granted to our sisters and attempt to appropriate it for ourselves. We drink from the wells they have dug in their struggles but often, as we do so, we choke the source from which life springs.

> When she looked at the baby she said 'This is a child of one of the Hebrews'. The child's sister who was watching said: 'Shall I find a nurse among the Hebrew women to suckle it?' 'Yes go' said Pharaoh's daughter and the child went off to find the baby's own mother.

God does not always grant us growth. Sometimes growth luxuriates in one place, whilst another is barren and bleak. Perhaps it is best to picture God working with two hands. One bestows life, another death.

Like Pharaoh's daughter white middle class women realize we have much to offer the endangered baby of our estranged sister – the creative energy she has given birth to in these barren times. We may feel drawn to promote its interest and advancement, we see we can use our privilege to give it the things that we enjoy. We can become its surrogate mother. Better able to care for it than its natural parent ever could. But we are in danger of forgetting the child is not an orphan. It has its own mother. It needs her milk not our honey.

> When the baby's mother came the daughter of Pharaoh said 'take the child away and suckle it for me. I will see that you are paid'.

But we are not without our uses. Pharaoh's daughter in the ancient story dwells at the very heart of the system the baby in the basket will challenge. A child of her own born of privilege and power would not have been able to bring liberation to the captive slaves. Had she taken and reared him in the place of her own baby, as a surrogate, he would not have been nourished with the knowledge and resilience his mother passed to him. He would have lost his Hebrew identity and been cut off from the source of life and growth he needed to sustain him.

Nevertheless the crying child in the basket is not to be passed by. Pharaoh's daughter may not claim it as her own but she can use her resources to see that its own mother has the possibility of giving it the care and nurture it requires. She can make space, she can give shelter and support. Power, money and privilege in this story are used wisely, used well. Used by the hands of God to bring life and death as the two hands of God at work so often do.

The time comes when the child suckled by the Hebrew woman and sustained by the Egyptian is old enough to enter the palace. It walks through the stone corridors, sees the fine ornaments and tastes the rich food. But it is old enough now and strong enough and wise enough to know that this is not the place of life and growth.

Pharaoh's daughter has brought to the centre of power a force that will destroy its dominion. The sons of Egypt will be struck down. It is a terrible thing to help to pull down the pillars of your own palace but sometimes God does not give us the role of bringing life but sharing in the destruction of what must die. Pharaoh's daughter has a difficult part to play but she plays it well. Because of it she is honoured in choosing the name of the baby in the basket, the liberator and destroyer. She is able to say, not that he is her own child, no not that, but that it was she who drew him out of the water when she heard his cry.

Heather Walton

PASSION FOR JUSTICE

Exodus 1; Luke 18.1–8

The story of Florence Siddons made headline news. It was the story of a woman who for thirteen years had fought for justice against the man she believed killed her grand-daughter. Although the courts had failed to convict him of the crime, she maintained her certainty that he was guilty. She pursued her case through various courts, drawing attention to her cause through petitions and protest marches, and involving family, friends and neighbours in money-raising activities in order to pay the legal bills. She finally won the right to sue him for damages in the civil courts.

You may have, as I did, all kinds of questions raised by that story. You may wonder about the legal issues of someone being sued for damages when attempts to secure a criminal conviction have failed. You may wonder about the psychological effects on that woman and her family of this struggle dominating their lives for several years. You may even wonder whether she is right to be so certain of this man's guilt. Yet what that story speaks of, unquestionably and unambiguously, is a consuming passion to see justice done, a passion for justice that takes over a person's life, becomes the directing force of her action.

It reminds me of that other story of a persistent woman, that we find in Luke chapter 18 – the story of a woman pestering a reluctant judge to take action on her behalf. It is a story that has frequently caused some embarrassment in Christian interpretation and preaching. How can we compare our loving, just God to this rather bureaucratic official who will give in if you nag hard enough, if only in order to get rid of you? Often the best that we have been able to do is a rather feeble 'Well, if even an unjust judge will respond in this way, how much more will a loving God' – which is a far cry from the vividness and directness of most of the parables of Jesus.

The problem arises because, as in so many androcentric readings of biblical texts, we have focussed on the man in the story rather than on the woman. We have seen the judge as a model of God, rather than seeing the woman as a model of salvation. It is *her* persistence, *her* dogged desire for justice, *her* refusal to accept oppression, which is held up as a model. This is how God's salvation, God's liberation comes – not through the reluctant assent of the powerful, but through the faithfulness and determination of the oppressed.

The picture of the woman is a picture of God's people holding on in faith – in the face of poverty, in the face of discrimination, in the face of indifference and neglect. It is a picture of the continued demand for justice and liberation.

Justice does not come easily. There are times when no one else seems to listen or care; there are times when the forces of oppression or injustice seem more powerful than any resources of faith or hope we can draw on; there are times when the relentless struggle makes our own vision and determination weaken. Whether we are struggling against poverty and unemployment in the face of increasingly-punitive government policies and legislation, whether we are resisting the constant ignoring or trivialization of women in the media, whether we are seeking to expose the hidden violation and abuse of children and the scandal of sexual violence, the story of the woman gives us encouragement. It is an encouragement not to give up: to continue in that persistent, patient, yet always impatient, demand for justice through which salvation comes.

But it is also more than an encouragement to perseverance; it is an affirmation that it is in that kind of demand, that kind of refusal to settle for injustice, that God's saving activity can be discerned. At the end of the story comes the question: 'When the Son of man comes, will he find faith on earth? The question implies that it is in the refusal to accept injustice, the refusal to submit to authority, that authentic faith and liberation are found.

An edition of the programme 'Out' on Channel 4 showed a clip of members of 'Outrage' disrupting a service at Westminster Abbey in protest at the Vatican's support for discrimination against gay people in certain areas of life and employment. Where, I asked myself, was faith to be found in that incident – in the quiet murmur of prayer and solemn organ music, or in the shouts and banners and posters affirming the dignity and worth of gay people, and their refusal to be silenced by ecclesiastical authority? I believe that it is in the affirmation of human value and dignity – of women, of black people, disabled people, gay people – that we can discern the same demand for justice, the same insistent claim for action, that is modelled for us by the woman in Jesus' story. In this kind of confrontation of indifference or oppression with the demands of justice, we see the faith on earth which the gospel requires of us.

Sometimes the action which we must take against injustice is clear and unambiguous; sometimes it is easy to identify the enemy and make a stand; sometimes we do not fear reprisals because we have nothing left to lose. But it is not always so easy for us to make our choices. In the story of the Hebrew midwives in the book of Exodus, we find a different picture.

The opening of Exodus describes a situation of oppression – one which is life-threatening, with the Hebrew people seemingly powerless in the grip of tyrannical authority. The story of the people breaking free of that oppression has been one of inspiration and hope. The metaphor of exodus has been a dominant one in much liberation theology, in its challenging of political and economic oppression. It has been a key metaphor too for many feminists who have left the church and the Christian tradition: from the famous exodus sermon of Mary Daly onwards there have been those who reach the conclusion that the church is irredeemably patriarchal and that to leave it is to escape from bondage.

The story of the Hebrew midwives offers a different strategy for defiance – a defiance that takes place within the system itself. When ordered to kill all male Hebrew children at birth the midwives do not argue or protest; instead they give the appearance of co-operation and use the opportunity quietly to subvert the system. I love to picture these women appearing before the Pharaoh, and protesting ingenuously that these Hebrew women deliver their babies far too quickly for them to intervene! It is a story of those who appear to co-operate, who work within the system, but continue to pursue their own values and to subvert from within.

There are many of us who work within structures where our basic values are challenged. In the health service, in education, in the public sector where efficiency, the imposition of cuts, and the need to make ever-greater savings prevent us from offering the kind of service that human dignity and worth requires; in national or local or even campaign politics where truth is concealed or compromised; in industry or commerce where the profit motive takes precedence over ethical or personal considerations. As the god of economic growth and the philosophy of the marketplace gain the ascendancy in so many spheres of our society it becomes increasingly difficult to raise questions of value or morality in anything other than personal terms. In such situations many are faced with difficult choices. It seems often as if the choice is to leave or to collude; but the story of the Hebrew midwives offers a different option – to remain within and to use what openings we have, the room for manoeuvre that is there if we look for it, in order to subvert the system and share in the process of liberation.

Sometimes these difficult questions face us even within the church – the place and the community where we would hope that our values of justice and freedom are affirmed and honoured as being at the core of the gospel of Christ. For many women these questions are raised most acutely by the feminist challenge: can the male symbols of God, the male dominance of church hierarchies, the refusal to recognize the ministry of women, be fought from within, or is the only option that has any integrity about it to leave an institution which has been, and continues to be, so oppressive? But similar questions arise in other contexts too – where we find the integrity of gay and lesbian relationships concealed through fear of ecclesiastical reprisals, where we find self-interest and a concern for 'growth' taking precedence over a bias for the poor – wherever we find the core gospel values of justice and inclusiveness and acceptance denied or undermined. In such a context we are faced with hard and difficult choices – do we remain within institutions and structures which deny our faith and undermine our values, or do we leave?

For many, the choice is that of exodus – to seek a promised land elsewhere, even if the journey is through the wilderness – and that is a right and appropriate, even though painful, choice for many. But the midwives offer us another strategy – that subversion from within that makes the eventual liberation possible. It is not an easy option – it carries with it all the ambiguities and tension which are inherent in living with contradiction – but it is the subversion from within that makes the eventual dramatic liberation possible.

In the narrative of the exodus story it is the subversive action of the midwives – followed by the equally risky actions of Moses' mother and sister – which enable the survival of the baby who is eventually to become the liberating leader. It would be tempting to see these as 'male' and 'female' roles complementing one another – but that would be to accept the androcentric bias of the biblical text! The two strategies – the subversion from within and the challenge of exodus – are interdependent: both are essential to the process of liberation. And it is the reality of our experience that the two go together; there are those working quietly, subtly, strategically for change from within, and there are those who mount the dramatic, revolutionary challenge. Too often we oppose one against the other – those who work for change and reform from within accuse those who leave of separatism and withdrawal; those who leave accuse those who stay of collusion and compromise. Both strategies require commitment and courage; both are costly, and both have their part to play in the movement towards freedom for which we long and to which the gospel calls us. I am convinced that the women's movement – and any movement for justice in the context of the structures of patriarchal church and society – needs both. The transformation and freedom of liberation is born of, in a sense midwived by, the patient, often hidden but none the less costly and risky, struggle from within.

Justice is often elusive; and our passion for justice is unlikely to be satisfied. We achieve a little here, and then become aware of injustice elsewhere; we gain some ground and then experience a backlash. But the two stories – of the persistent woman and the Hebrew midwives – give us hope: that in the process of pestering and persisting, that in living with tension and contradiction, we are sharing in the activity of the liberating God.

Jan Berry

GOOD FRIDAY

The liturgy for Good Friday in the Russian Orthodox Church ends with a long reading from the Book of Job, from the last chapter where Job is restored to prosperity after his sufferings. This choice of the book of Job to say something about Good Friday is important. Job is the story of a prosperous and successful man, a man of faith, a good man, whose faith is tested to the uttermost. In a series of catastrophes, which are mysteriously orchestrated from heaven, he loses all his wealth. His children all die in hideous accidents. He is left with his wife, and in one of the oldest misogynist jokes on earth, this turns out to be more a curse than a blessing. He is finally afflicted with a revolting skin disease. Three friends, who have all done the latest course in pastoral counselling, come to visit him. After sitting with him in silence and after appropriate expressions of sympathy they begin to try to help. Don't you think it's possible, they begin to say, tentatively at first and then more insistently, that you may have brought this on yourself? Don't you think it's just possible that God is trying to tell you something? Don't you think you could, perhaps, change your attitude a bit? Review your life? Think more positively?

All of which, I am glad to tell you, Job steadfastly refuses to do. He is outraged by what has happened to him. He insists that God explains himself. He complains without interruption for almost half of the forty-odd chapters, as his pious friends try to persuade him to take a more moderate position and to reconcile himself to his fate. But Job will not be reconciled. Faced with the trial of his own faith he suggests that God should appear in court to explain himself, even though the only judge, prosecutor and defendent would have had to be God himself. The argument goes round and round in rather tedious circles. Now and then we get a hint that something important is being said, that some new kind of wisdom is on the point of breaking through. That some hidden twist of the plot is about to turn all the arguments on their heads. And then, quite suddenly, in the thirty-eighth chapter, it does. God speaks to Job out of the whirlwind.

'Where were you when I laid the foundations of the earth?' God does not answer Job's complaint at all. He never meets his anxieties or deals with his criticisms. But he does appear, he does speak. He is present to him. What God does is to show Job the universe of his creation. The stars, the sea with its tides, the day and the night, the rain, the wild creatures of the earth, the ostrich, the hawk and the horse. Faced with all this Job is silenced. But it is not a submissive silence. It is the silence of awe.

Job's suffering and his refusal to deny it or trivialize it, or moralize it, has brought about a revelation. God takes him right into the heart of the creation, into the heart of the creative process, into a universe of spinning worlds, of change, of chaos and creativity, beauty and suffering. It is the world that the sub-atomic physicist sees, a world of order and disorder, life and death, bound together inextricably.

And once the cosmic show has begun God does not stop it. Even when Job has lapsed into silence God does not stop. He shows Job two mighty creatures, a huge beast of the land, and a scaly beast of the sea. They are a translator's nightmare – most settle for the hippopotamus and the crocodile, but the likelihood is that they are intended to be mythical creatures, monsters like dragons, symbols of chaos. God invites Job to put a ring through the earth monster's nose and take it for a walk. Then to throw a fishing rod into the ocean and draw out the beast of the sea. Go on, God seems to be saying, you run this universe then. You tame my wild beasts that give me joy. You moralize and pontificate and organize things and make this a good safe world where no one gets hurt, and where there is no wildness and no wonder. Go on, here's your chance!

It is a chance that Job declines to take up. The revelation of God's strange wisdom in creation leaves him dumbstruck. 'I had heard of thee by the hearing of an ear', he says, 'But now my eye sees thee'.

The difference between hearing and seeing is what tranforms Job. What he sees is the beauty, the creativity of this astonishing universe. What he sees is a God of galaxies, of particles that hover on the edge of existence, of crystalline structures, each unique, of the slow building of a coastline and the buckling of the earth to produce a mountain range. What he sees is a God who rejoices in the stamping horse and protects the foolish ostrich, who watches with the hawk and leaps with the mountain goat. Yes, and a God whose creation can produce the terrible volcanic lava flow that engulfs villages and destroys lives. The chaos monsters, too, are part of God's creation.

And God speaks not as a mechanic who has invented a clockwork machine, to run predictably until the end of time, but as a poet who weaves worlds like words, an artist, a dancer, God the mother in labour with worlds, God the Trinity of encircling suns, God, the depth and ground of being.

This is not a safe world, says the book of Job. It is not even, or always a good world. But it is a deeply interesting world, a world in which we can speak to God, and be heard, a world open to God in every particle and molecule.

The end of the book of Job has the hero restored to himself, his illness is healed, his wealth is doubled, he has seven sons and three daughters, and the daughters are named, and receive the inheritance along with their brothers. (The feminist implications of which I am sure I need not draw your attention to.)

So our eastern orthodox brothers and sisters end Good Friday on this note of restoration and hope. As one of the ancient writers put it, 'All things are altered by thy passion', the whole creation is restored and renewed by what happens on the cross. And our vision of it, too, is transformed.

Job prepares us to see suffering, not as an anomaly, but as something built in, something necessary for the creativity of the world. Something, too, which God shares with us. I know this is difficult. We always want to moralize because it lets us off the hook. What have I done, we instinctively say, when disaster strikes, What have I done to deserve this? My God, why? We cannot quite believe in the audacity of the creation, that the randomness should go so deep, that death and chance are part of God's holy and divine order. That the cross itself symbolizes the law of sacrifice that runs through creation. This is not an amoral universe. There is a moral balance, but it is not worked out as we might expect. In this dazzling universe the foolish and the guilty are carried by the innocent and the good. The total cost is underwritten by God himself. God pays the price in full. And this is, I think what Job understands at the end of the book.

Would we rather live in a perfect world? Sometimes, if we are honest, probably yes. But a perfect world, Job suggests, is a dead world, a world incapable of change.

Think of a bunch of flowers, selected, picked, cut, arranged. A lovely gift, a decoration. You would not expect to find sickly or wrinkled blooms among them because they have been chosen one by one. Job's counsellors assumed that God's world is as contrived as that bunch of flowers. They looked for that kind of coherence in the world. They assumed that only the beautiful is the chosen, what is unbeautiful, diseased or bereaved, has somehow fallen short of God's design. It is not willed. It must either cure itself or drop out of creation. There are many designer spiritualities which teach this kind of thing today, some of them Christian, banging on about wholeness and healing as if they were vitamins you could swallow and wash down with prayer.

The tree of life is not like that. The tree that lasts is rooted in the earth. It has to fight for its existence. Against the internal hazards of its own growth, the things that can go wrong with its cells and its structure, and against the external hazards of rough weather, poor soil. When it is grown you can see what its been through. There will be broken branches, injured bark, bruised leaves. The shrivelled, faded parts, even the dead bits, are, on the tree, in their rightful place. They reflect the struggle of the trunk in attaining its own growth.

The Jesuit palaeontologist Pere Teilhard de Chardin, used this image of the tree in a paper he wrote in a Catholic journal for those who work with people with long term illnesses. He goes on:

> The world is an immense groping, an immense search. It can only progress at the cost of many failures, many casualties', and then he comes to the heart of it, 'The sufferers (in spite of what they may often feel) are not useless or diminished elements. They are merely those who pay the price of the universe's progress, and in doing so, triumph. It is exactly those who bear in their enfeebled bodies and minds the weight of the moving world who find themselves the most active factors in that very process which seems to sacrifice and shatter them.

Those who bear the weight of this moving world. The rejected, the dismissed, the unwanted ones. They are the ones who find themselves the active factors in the very process which seems to sacrifice and shatter them.

I have found myself thinking about Teilhard's tree often, once in a mental hospital, once in the intensive care unit of a hospital, once when meeting a group of people with the most severe learning disabilities. I have thought of it also when listening to people whose lives have gone wrong, victims of others' violence or betrayal. And yet the words are nothing.

On all these occasions I was there as an outsider, a film-maker, a collector of images to be frozen in time. My detachment was necessary. But there have been other times, as there will have been for you, when I have not been an outsider. When the person in intensive care belongs to you, when it is your own life that is being broken apart by carelessness, callousness or wickedness. And then the words that try to reach and comprehend seem pious and unreal. Within the experience there is nothing at all to hold on to. Suffering is always the trial of faith, as it was for Job. The cross of Jesus is where faith is tried to the uttermost and there is no sign of fruit in that barren and blasted tree, as the Son of God dies and the heavens themselves go dark. I do not know what makes this pain fruitful. There are hints in the natural world, the secrecy of the seed, the cosmic destructions that lead to galaxies, the fragmenting of stars that pour out the elements of life. But that is not what it looks like while you stand by watching your love and your life in pain, labouring to live or die. And then I think again of Mary, the Mother of God, helpless to do anything but stand there. She cannot save him, she must just stay there and not run away, but somehow hold the mystery in his dying in her heart as she once held the mystery of his conception in her womb.

I don't know what the resurrection is or how it happens, but it does happen. Yet when you're in the middle of it it is no help at all. I think of Helen Waddell, that marvellous Irish woman who wrote the story of Peter Abelard, and gave us the image of the world as God's cross. She saw the suffering of God running right through creation, like the rings on the inside of a tree trunk. Calvary, she says, is the bit we saw, where the trunk of a fallen tree is sliced through. Thirty years later Helen Waddell died in a London hospital of a slow brain disease which gradually robbed her of all her sparkling intelligence, her memory, her relationships, even her understanding of faith.

Her biographer, a Benedictine nun, Felicitas Corrigan, tells us how as her mind went she simply sat every day before a picture of Christ crucified. And she asks, as perhaps only a contemplative, would ask 'in that darkness of soul and body, who shall say what mighty work was being wrought?'.

We see in such illness only the waste and tragedy, and we are right to see them, but the eye of faith, without denying that, can sometimes see more. That such suffering can be offered. That it can be, perhaps, used. Not justified, but used. Today we say that the world is redeemed by a helpless man, pinned hand and foot to a cross.

Few of us are called to bear great pain, but even the messy confusions of our lives can take us towards the shadow of the cross, the tree of life. The death of a relationship, divorce, illness – these are the mortifications which put us in touch with the cross. When my own marriage broke up I was angry and depressed for the best part of a decade. I was driven inward to look at the sources of depression in the half-forgotten twilight world of childhood. There was nothing particularly dreadful, just the twists and turns and emotional bumps and bruises that go on in many families. I worked, made films about depression and feminism and the nuclear bomb and the future of the Church of England, and other deeply serious, grim sort of subjects. I went on retreat and prayed a lot, and thought about becoming a nun. Briefly, though – a friend pointed out that I would miss my gin and tonic!

A strange thing happened one Holy Week. It was the custom in our church to keep a watch all through the night. I signed up for 3 a.m. When I arrived the candles were low and guttering. The daffodils stood stark in their vases. A long time passed. Then I heard the most extraordinary noise coming from outside. I couldn't think what it was. It was relentless, inhuman, instinctive. And I suddenly knew. It was the birds. It was a spring morning and the birds were awake singing with inhuman joy that the light would come. There was not a shred of light in the sky. But the birds knew that the light would come.

The creation itself, the creation that doesn't know what else to do but praise the creator in what it is and does, witnessed to the rebirth of light. To me that morning the birds were like angels, in human messengers of a grace and freedom still to come.

That Good Friday morning I began to see the cross not as an answer to the problem of suffering but as an icon of what it means to live in God's world. There is the tree that shatters human wisdom, that gives life, that restores relationships, that joins earth to heaven.

The tree of life my soul has seen, laden with fruit and always green.

I think this is something to hold on to in the complexities of our life, in our anxiety, in our scepticism and in our suffering. In all these things God shares with us something of the burden of creation, the wound of knowledge that comes with being conscious and aware. God has not abandoned us, nor has God abandoned this world. He calls on us to rise from our despair to know that there is a Heart at the heart of this universe, and that the name of the heart is love.

Angela Tilby

3

Speaking from the Text

Most preachers have been taught about the Bible and learned their lessons well. They have been taught that they must always begin with the Bible, that the sermon is not the place to ponder in public your own private thoughts, but the momentous speech in which the word of God, made known in the Bible and preeminently in the person of Jesus Christ, is proclaimed for God's people today. The preacher, often gowned to make clear his or her representational role, draws the attention of the congregation to the deepest insights of the Bible. This Bible, even seen through the lens of modern scholarship, is the prime authority for faith – the good book with pages worth adorning with gold and the starting place for all good preachers. More modestly perhaps, good liberal Christians will speak of the Bible as the 'classic' text among Christians, the foundation document for faith.

Preachers are taught that the Bible is a good book. Even the uncomfortable passages – the 'eye for an eye' morality, the stories of rape and abuse and human sacrifice, the boring genealogies, the propaganda and the hysteria – even these are helpful because they enable us to say of the Bible that 'all of life is here'. Preachers are taught that, even though it is a library of books varying in their origin, content and style, the Bible has such an underlying unity that one part of it can be used as a kind of cipher for interpreting another, that the Old Testament comes to life in the light of the New. Preachers are also taught how to interpret the Bible. They learn that exegesis (getting the meaning out of the text) is good, but that eisegesis (reading your meaning in) is bad. They learn to value above all the 'plain meaning' of the text, to despise allegorical interpretation or any reading which seems contrary to the intention of the author. They learn to preach 'good news' with clarity and forcefulness in order to strengthen faith among those who listen.

This is, of course, a parody, but parody depends for its truth upon the grains of truth which remain like an irritant when the laughter is past. In some places, and notably among women, many of these commonly passed on assumptions about preaching and the Bible have come into question. The Bible may be a book of God, but can we go on preaching from it as though in every case, if only one could get to the 'real' meaning, something good can be found in every text?

Liturgical committees devising lectionaries struggle to find more significant and affirming passages about women – to make women visible. But it is not only the invisibility of women that has been the problem with the Bible. Must we not also recognize that many biblical texts deny the real humanity of women and are texts which have fed and strengthened some of the most appalling sexism throughout the history of Christendom? Does not the dark side of scripture need to be named and not simply covered up by a more judicious choice of passages to be read in church?

The misogyny of many of our literary classics is now well catalogued by feminist critics and feminist biblical scholars have also done their work (see for example, Phyllis Trible's *Texts of Terror*), but this naming of misogyny has also begun to find its place in the pulpit. No longer can we go on saying 'Amen' every time the scripture is read. This revealing of the darkness, this naming of oppression, will not sound like the 'good news' we have been taught to proclaim, but how could it be anything other than good, to name the suffering of the past and the present and in naming it to long for its end? So, part of what it means to preach as a woman is to name the misogyny of the Bible and to resist it from the pulpit. It is to recognize that it is not always a 'good book'. It is to challenge the authority of a collection of texts which has provided a very significant spur and encouragement to our oppressors, naming us as 'helpmeet' and bidding us be silent and secondary. The Bible may be a source of liberation for many, but it is also a text of terror.

As well as naming its oppressive power, women who preach have begun to recognize that it is not true to say of the Bible that 'all of life is there'. In the Bible we do find stories that recognize some of the complexity of human living. The biblical characters are not plaster saints and you have only to read the letters of Paul to discover that the early church was not a community without its problems. The Bible presents us with the strange muddle of the sublime and the dreadful, the unspeakable and the unspoken that is humankind open to God. But, the stories are told and the letters are written and the laws are proclaimed and the psalms are prayed by *male* narrators and from their point of view. The main performers of the Bible texts are male, with barely a few cameo roles for women. All of life is not there, because these are texts written by, and largely for, men. The story of the women lies untold.

Naturally, this has consequences for preaching. The feminist reader of novels can take the option to turn away from the largely male canon of 'good books' and read instead books written by women, but the feminist preacher cannot turn so simply to an alternative canon. However, there are a number of possibilities open to us. We can use strategies of interpretation which enable us to hear the women's voices which have been silenced by the canon and by the text. Women can, of course, preach on the texts that there are about women; the conversion of Lydia rather than the conversion of Paul, Martha's confession of faith rather than Peter's. But this strategy has its limitations and, of course, even these texts are written by men and with an androcentric (man-centred) bias.

An alternative strategy lies in preaching on a text in which a woman (or women) appears on the margins and re-reading the text from her point of view. How does the story of Abraham sound if Sarah tells it? What does Mary feel as, fleeing the city, she stops for a moment to look back on the slaughter of the innocents? Who are the women named almost in passing in his letters as Paul's co-workers? To what kind of early church do they bear witness?

To ask these kinds of questions of the text will lead us to preach in new ways. We will be accused, of course, of eisegesis, of 'reading in' our own thoughts and bending the text to our own will. But the idea that texts are fixed and stable entities containing clear and fixed meanings has long been questioned. To read is always to engage in a creative interchange between text and reader, both of which are more shifting and moving in their identities than many would have us believe. All texts are multi-layered and brim-full of interpretive potential – there are new readings to be had in abundance and women preachers may glean a rich harvest from the often alien corn. We may preach from what is unsaid as well as what is said, from the margins rather than the centre, from the hidden history and the silent witnesses. Since the most 'obvious' meaning of the text (or even the intended meaning) is never the only possible one, we may read a text 'against the grain'. We can 'deconstruct' it and show how new readings are struggling to be found. Can we read the story of Eve 'against' itself – seeing her not as foolish and weak but as the strong one searching for wisdom? Can we question the central story of the Exodus God, by letting the side stories of the conquest of the Canaanites and their goddesses subvert the centre? In such ways the Bible may become again a source of liberation.

The preacher who is a woman must learn to read the Bible again, and to read as a woman. We have been taught to read as men and the texts construct their ideal reader as male. At many points the reader is addressed as 'brother' and is assumed to have the concerns of men. We have learned to accept the male point of view as the norm and the female one as marginal or even deviant. However, women can learn to become resisting readers, readers who refuse to be the reader that the text (or author) intends. We will take some measure of control of what we read and our eyes, being opened to the deceptions and distortions of our fathers, will light on new things.

Many of these ideas could be illustrated by reference to sermons throughout the book, as most of the sermons included bear some relation to the Bible. However, of those particularly chosen for this section, a number of strategies can be observed. Margaret Hebblethwaite provides a meditation on one of the well known biblical passages about a woman; the Samaritan woman at the well; the foreign, divorced housewife before whom Jesus announces his Messiahship. Janet Martin Soskice and Hazel Addy both write from their experience as women but, while Janet Martin Soskice draws affirmation from positive strands within the text Hazel Addy discovers liberation in anger and resistance to the text as she names new models for God. Elizabeth

Templeton ponders hermeneutical questions, by focussing on the history of the interpretation of the figure of Rahab and of the 'theological pleasure' which readers have taken from her. Susan Durber re-reads and re-writes the story of the three wise men, refusing to allow the dark side of the story to be hidden from us, refusing to settle for the male point of view. Alison Peacock re-tells the story of the foreign woman who changes Jesus' mind – her imaginative, narrative sermon gives us a sense of the 'danger' of the story.

I THIRST

John 19.28

For the second time in John's Gospel, Jesus is thirsty. As we watch Jesus struggle through minute after minute of these long three hours, our mind goes back to earlier memories, when he was strong and active and following him seemed an endless happiness.

One such memory is of Jesus in Samaria, in the midday sun, sitting on the edge of a well, with no bucket to scoop up the water. A woman came to draw water, and Jesus spoke to her, 'Give me a drink.' He approached her as someone thirsty, someone in need of what she could give him.

But as the conversation continued he let her know what he had to offer. 'If you knew the gift of God, and who it is that is saying to you, "Give me a drink" you would have asked him, and he would have given you living water.' It is a theme Jesus picks up later, in the temple, as he cries out, 'If any are thirsty, let them come to me and drink. Those who believe in me, as the scripture has said, "Out of their heart shall flow rivers of living water."'

The Samaritan woman, weary from having to fetch water in the midday heat, like so many other women throughout history, worn down by household tasks that they cannot get others to share, leapt at the possibility of a lightening of her load. 'Sir, give me this water, that I may not thirst, nor come here to draw.'

At first Jesus appeared to change the subject, as though to

avoid granting her request, but in a couple more minutes he gave that living water in an unexpected way: he told her who he was. She said, 'I know that Messiah is coming ... when he comes he will show us all things.' Jesus answered, 'I who speak to you am he.'

This might not be surprising were it not for the fact that Jesus never tells people he is the Messiah. So closely guarded is the messianic secret, that Jesus enforces vows of secrecy on those who guess it. He does not even tell Peter – he waits till Peter tells him, before confirming his belief.

Yet there he was, actually announcing that he was the Messiah. It is one of the greatest privileges in the Gospels, and it was granted to a woman, a mere housewife, and a foreigner, and a divorcee.

And by doing that he turned her into an apostle. 'The woman left her water jar, and went away into the city, and said to the people, "Come, see a man who told me all that I ever did."' In an extraordinary way he had granted her the gift of the spring of water flowing within and welling up to eternal life, and he had granted it to a woman even as she slaved over her household tasks, making her an apostle to the men, even as after his resurrection Mary Magdalene was to be sent as an apostle to the apostles with the news of the resurrection.

This memory flashes through our mind, and as we stay at the foot of the cross we notice how many around us are women: 'There were also many women there, looking on from afar, who had followed Jesus from Galilee, ministering to him; among whom were Mary Magdalene, and Mary the mother of James and Joseph, and the mother of the sons of Zebedee (Matt. 27.55–6). Just as we notice how many in this church are women.

And we remember how it was a woman, and one who was overburdened with domestic work, and foreign, and divorced, that Jesus first privileged by saying to her 'I, who speak to you, am he'. And we who are women thank him for the way he treated us, as Jesus stirs our memory, crying out, in echo of that earlier occasion, 'I thirst'.

Margaret Hebblethwaite

ANNUNCIATION*

Luke 1.26–38

The Feast of the Annunciation on 25 March is a wondrous and fruitful feast in the middle of the rather gloomy season of Lent.

Of course, the Annunciation isn't intended to be light relief from Lent. It's dating is determined in an almost bare-facedly biological way: 25 March is exactly nine months before 25 December. This points to one of the delightful things about the annunciation and about Marian theology in general – it's a strange mixture of the most exalted of Christian mysteries and the most human of human events, as I shall try to show.

In my investigations, I have discovered an interesting anomaly. The *Oxford University Diary*, that organ of rectitude, refers to this feast as 'the Annunciation of the Blessed Virgin Mary' – whereas the much less prestigious *Westminster Diocesan Year Book* calls it 'the Annunciation of the Lord'. Now, I know that the *Oxford Diary* is always right, or at least fastidiously correct, but in this case I'd plump for the *Westminister Diocesan Year Book*. For annunciation means announcement, and the announcement in question is not really the announcement of the Blessed Virgin Mary, but the announcement to the Blessed Virgin Mary, in fact, the announcement of our Lord to the Blessed Virgin Mary. Calling it 'the Annunciation of the Lord' seems to me to get the balance right because the feast, like all Marian feasts (and all Marian theology properly understood) is about the Lord. It is a feast of incarnation.

I started to think more seriously about the Annunciation after falling on some interesting remarks Thomas Aquinas makes about it. In a text no doubt familiar to you all, volume 51 of the *Summa Theologiae*, Aquinas says this:

> Next we have to examine the announcement to the Blessed Virgin. Here are four points of inquiry;

---

* A sermon given at Ripon College, Cuddesdon in March 1984.

1. Was it right for her to be told about who would be born of her?
2. Who ought to have told her?
3. In what manner?
4. Was the announcement well planned?

These sound like inquiries more appropriate to Debrett's *Book of Etiquette* than to a text of theology, but Aquinas has some interesting things to say, particularly about the *manner* in which the announcement was made to Mary. Of this he asks,

> Should the angel of the annunciation have appeared bodily (that is, visually) to the Virgin?

After all, as Augustine and the mystics tell us, physical visions are a low grade of religious experience. The mystics tell us that crude physical signs like these are usually given to those who are too weak to do without them and surely Mary wasn't one such. But, says Aquinas, in Mary's case it was entirely fitting that the angel appeared to her bodily, not because she was spiritually under-developed, but because a bodily revelation was consonant with the message itself – for the angel came to tell of the *incarnation* (the becoming flesh) of the *visible* God. The sensible nature of the appearance to Mary points to the actual appearance of the Son of God in the flesh. Mary was able to receive the Son of God in her womb as well as in her mind.

I am reminded of those early Italian paintings of the Annunciation – the stylized ones where you see, on the one side, Mary sitting in a pavilion surrounded by symbols of wisdom and purity (books and lilies and so on), and on the other side you see the Angel Gabriel with his hand raised in greeting. Between them, usually in gold lettering, you see actual Latin words written in, words which run from the angel's mouth to the Virgin's midriff. I had always imagined paintings like these were visual aids for illiterate church goers, as we're told stained glass windows were meant to be, and that the words were there so that everyone would know what occasion the painting depicted. But of course not! In the Annunciation the *Word became flesh*, and so, of course, the painters have made *the words physically there* in the painting just as the word was physically there in the annunciation itself. The annunciation wasn't just a conceptual thing, but a very concrete one.

This understood, Luke's account of the annunciation is an imprimatur for painters and for all representative Christian art. God did not scorn to come in the flesh and because of this we can now represent him in earthly materials. (I believe the Orthodox Church's theology of icons draws explicitly on this incarnational line of thought.) Here again, is this odd mixture of the pretty mysterious and the close to earth.

Luke's account of the annunciation is an equally rich mixture of the literary, the typological, the putatively biographical – to my mind we should see it as a theological *construction* in which Luke not only alludes to Old Testament parallels, but weaves in the 'christological language and formulas of the post-resurrection church'. So, Luke's infancy narratives, we are told, 'abound in echoes of Abraham and Sarah, of David's description of Gabriel, of the Samson story, of the promise to David, of the (other) annunciations – of birth patterns'. Luke's actual format of the annunciation follows patterns seen in annunciations to Zechariah, to Abraham, to Moses and Gideon. Some have claimed that the portrayal of Mary here echoes back to female portrayals of Wisdom in the Old Testament, and have suggested that the angelic mode of greeting – 'Rejoice, highly favoured one' is intended to evoke the Old Testament female personification of Israel or Zion. Mary is thus depicted in the infancy narrative as a type of the new Israel, the church.

Some Roman Catholic interpretations have also understood that Luke, in the infancy narratives, alludes to a comparison between Mary and the Ark of the Covenant. In Luke 1.35, the angel says, 'The power of the Lord will *overshadow* you'. This same verb is used in the Greek version of Old Testament when the cloud of God's glory *overshadows* the Tabernacle in the desert, and the winged cherubim *overshadow* the Ark of the Covenant. So just as the Ark bore the Old Covenant in the tablets of the Law, so Mary bears the New Covenant, the living Covenant, in Christ. Whether this parallel with the Ark of the Covenant was intended by Luke or not, 'Ark of the Covenant' is a traditional Marian title;

Mystical rose,
Tower of David,
Tower of Ivory,
House of Gold,
Ark of the Covenant,
Gate of Heaven.

It has also been common for Roman Catholic theologians to understand Luke to be making this allusion in saying that 'when Elizabeth heard the greeting of Mary, the child leapt in her womb', for just as David danced before the old Ark (II Sam. 6.14), so John the Baptist, yet unborn, leaps in his mother's womb before the living Covenant in Christ. (Not much credence should be given to the idea that Luke intended this allusion, but it is food for thought.)

It is more probable, however, that Luke deliberately weaves into the birth narratives christological formulas of the post-resurrection church. Here too, the mention of 'overshadowing' in the annunciation is important for it echoes the 'overshadowing' of Luke 9.34 when, at the transfiguration, 'a cloud came and overshadowed them' and 'a voice came out of the cloud, saying, "This is my son, my Chosen, listen to him"'. Furthermore, the language of the angel's promise, 'The Holy Spirit will come upon you, and the power of the Holy Spirit will overshadow you, and therefore the child to be born will be called holy, the Son of God' has overt parallels to the language used of Jesus' baptism; 'and the Holy Spirit descended upon him in bodily form, as a dove, and a voice came from heaven, "Thou art my beloved Son, with thee I am well pleased"'. The significance of these parallels with baptism and transfiguration is that it would seem, for Luke, that the message of the annunciation contains a basic post-resurrectional proclamation of the Christian faith. *Mary* is being presented as the first one to hear the gospel, hence her prominence in the Lucan infancy narrative.

I haven't spoken very much about the person Mary – just as though she were some passive, shadowy figure whose only role was to act as a vehicle for all the typological abstractions. You might think this feast of incarnation isn't really about the person of Mary at all, but of course it absolutely is.

It was *Mary*, not a woman, but *this* woman Mary – this *person*

Mary, who accepted Christ into her life in the most intimate way imaginable. 'Behold, I am the handmaid of the Lord; let it be to me according to your word.' And this was not just a *passive* acceptance, but an active and deliberate and free choice. The church has always recognized that it is Mary's acceptance of God's will which is at the very heart of the theological importance of the Annunciation. As Augustine says, Mary is better for having conceived Christ in faith than in flesh – for Mary would have gained nothing from her physical and maternal nearness to Christ if she had not first conceived Christ in her heart.

Mary is the first Christian, the first one to hear the gospel, the first Christian disciple. She meets Luke's principle of ideal discipleship; that is 'to hear the word of God and to do it' (8.21, 15). This gives the key to the story, later in Luke, of the woman in the crowd who cries, 'Blessed is the womb that bore you, and the breasts that you sucked!"' But he said "Blessed rather are those who hear the word of God and keep it"' (Luke 11.27–28). The Eastern Orthodox Church has always maintained that in this passage, far from slighting Mary, Jesus indicates where her true glory lay – in her faithful response to God. Mary heard the word of God and kept it, in her mind and in her body.

As the first Christian, the first Christian disciple, Mary is the pattern for all Christians, for all human beings. For Christ becomes incarnate in each of us. As Gerard Manley Hopkins says,

> ... the just man justices,
> keeps grace, that keeps all his goings and graces;
> Acts in god's eyes what in God's eyes he is –
> Christ – for Christ plays in ten thousand places,
> Lovely in limbs, lovely in eyes not his
> To the Father through the features of men's faces.

If we look at Mary and see Christ this is not because Mary is unimportant. When we look at any human being (dead, stumbling, starving, sinning) we should see Christ – not just Christ so that Joe or Jane or Judith is cast away like a worthless husk, but in seeing Christ – the Joe or Jane or Judith that really *is*, for *to be* is to be in God.

Janet Martin Soskice

THE WOMAN WITH BLEEDING

Luke 8.41–56

I want to begin by sharing something of the history of my experience with this passage from Luke's Gospel.

From my childhood, I remember a Bible I had, King James version, paper, thin leaves, with a black cover. It had pictures in it. There was a picture of Jesus raising Jairus' daughter back to life. Jesus was reaching out to her, and she was rising from her bed, her arm stretched out to meet his. At the point where the tips of their fingers seemed to be touching, there was something that looked like it was meant to be electricity coming out from Jesus' finger ends. I remember being puzzled by the story. Even as a child I knew that dead people do not come back to life, but nevertheless I was intrigued by the nature of the power Jesus seemed to have. I also wondered about this other story of the women healed miraculously by Jesus.

I tried to relate it to my own experience to understand it. I belong to that generation of children which medical fashion robbed of their tonsils by the time they were five. I was ill for a long time afterwards and missed a lot of my first year at school. This was because, I remember my mother saying, after my operation, I had a haemorrhage. The King James version talks of the woman having a haemorrhage, and so I approached this story believing that the woman, like me, had had her tonsils out.

Moving from childhood to early adulthood, I then knew that the woman's problem was menstrual bleeding. There was nothing else it could be really. Although I heard preaching on the story, no preacher ever referred to this fact by name. But I wasn't really surprised, since by this time I had picked up that certain things weren't or couldn't be mentioned in God's house. I had picked up people's discomfort and embarassment with this story. I still wondered about this being raised from the dead business and the miraculous nature of the healing. Even though by this time I had made my profession of faith, an agnostic position was the best I could muster.

Moving on again to later in my life, when I was a student in biblical studies, I learned the language of rationalization. If I couldn't believe in miracles, there was a way round this. I could look behind the event being described for a message about the nature and power of God in Christ. This was acceptable because the Gospel writers had exercised literary licence in the first place, recording the truth as they saw it through story and metaphor. Similarly with Jairus' daughter, this may or may not actually have happened, I could make my own mind up about this particular resurrection. After all, she is not a really significant actor in the salvation drama. Not even her name is known. *The* resurrection was of course a different matter. In a theological college, you couldn't actually say of *the* resurrection that it didn't happen, only that it may not have happened quite like it's recorded. The question looms large. Is it possible that there are peculiar events, like resurrections and miracles, which interrupt the normal causal relationships persisting in nature and in history? To answer 'No, but' seems like religious fudge. A straight 'No', and the essence of Christianity would seem to crumble before my eyes. And to say 'Yes' is unthinkable.

But let me move quickly on to the present time. Philosophical questions about miracles still threaten to shatter the Christian pedestal under my feet. Nevertheless I have a renewed interest in stories like these, because they involve Jesus in encounters with women. Such stories are rare. They have, in recent years, been enthusiastically poured over by some Christian women seeking to establish sisterhood with our biblical sisters. The claim is that there is a common bond of experience and circumstance, in which the Jesus who was kind to women at a time when it is said that most men weren't, is claimed as the first feminist.

I have my reservations about that kind of enterprise but one positive aspect of it, is that it encourages you to see your own experience as an authority which can be brought to a Bible reading. As I try to do this with the reading from Luke, I find these questions arising.

First, I want to ask why it is that although I have heard sermons on these stories often enough before, I have never actually heard it said that the woman had a menstrual disorder. I have heard references to haemorrhages and euphemistic flows of blood. In the case of the girl, I have never actually heard it said that she was

the age of puberty. Here is experience and context that I can relate
to, and yet I have never heard it named in church. Maybe, I
wonder, this silence indicates a taboo. In Judaism, menstruating women were regarded as ritually taboo. In mediaeval
Christianity, such women were forbidden to receive communion,
and forbidden from ever touching holy objects or walking on
holy ground. We can laugh at this, isn't it wonderful that we don't
believe such things now. *But*, do the remnants of such ancient
taboos live on in the silence now? Do they live on in the acrimony
of those men and women who oppose the ordination of women to
the priesthood. Such taboos certainly live on in secular forms.
(You'll have heard these.) Women are totally dominated by their
hormones. They go bananas at the sight of a teapot or a baby.
This makes them (so the argument goes) unfit for exercising
responsible roles of power outside the home. In Jesus' day, such
taboos of religion, sex, and convention were firmly in place. The
child, being dead, was taboo, and the woman because of her
illness had the same status. She might as well have been dead. For
someone to touch either is to make themselves unclean. This
woman must have known the rules as well as anyone. She must
have known that the rules said she would spread her contamina-
tion if she touched another person. So for her to reach out and
touch Jesus must have taken a lot of guts. Both actions, that of the
woman, and that of Jesus when he touched the girl, both actions
cut across the taboo. They broke the taboo and they brought
healing. And so I wonder what it would be like if the silence or our
present-day taboos were to be broken: and what the possibilities
are for wholeness that we deny ourselves because we dare not
break taboo.

Second, I bring to the reading fairly strong feelings of anger.
Because I know that no amount of faith has ever brought a dead
child back to life, and no amount of faith can heal a gynaecological disorder. Those things just do not happen. And so I feel
angry because these stories are so, so cruel. In their suggestion
that faith can bring about miracles of healing, they cut across and
deny our human experience and our knowledge of the truth. And
they blame us, as victims, for supposed faithlessness. The last
thing any of us needs at times of vulnerability (or indeed at any
time) is for such callousness to be coming straight from the lips of

Jesus. The picture of God suggested is hardly one of a loving God. Just what kind of God would be so cruel as to suggest such things. If this is God, is this God really worth believing in?

And so, third, I have a need as a Christian to explore whether these stories are for me reclaimable, or whether the pain they cause in human experience is not so great as to suggest their excision from the body of teaching we have traditionally held to be authoritative.

My usual practice when I write a sermon is to look up a couple of Bible commentaries, not so much to look *for* something, but rather to minimize the risk of too many exegetical blunders. I noticed that commentators on all three versions of the woman story focus very much on Jesus as the star actor. They emphasize the control that Jesus had over his power, so that he knew he had been touched, even though dozens of people were crowding round him. Loathe as I am to disagree with that, I think that a straightforward reading of Luke's, and to a lesser extent Mark's version, clearly suggests that when the woman touched Jesus, something happened to Jesus which was *outside* his control, and that the woman immediately *healed herself*. Her healing was not granted as a reward for her honesty in coming forward afterwards, nor was it dependent on the words of Jesus. She touched him, and in so doing, she brought about her own healing. She did not ask permission 'Would it be OK with you Jesus?'. She knew what she needed and she took it. She literally helped herself. Proverb: God helps those who help themselves but God help them who are caught helping themselves. Jesus doesn't reprimand. Rather he says something like 'Good on you!'. She took, and Jesus says 'Well done'.

For the woman to take, given her cultural and medical background, must have taken enormous courage and showed tremendous faith – in *herself*. In our culture, women are traditionally seen as passive, being given to, being done to. We are taught not to take for ourselves because this is selfish. An article on the *Guardian*'s women's page began with a quotation from the writer's school report. 'She is a bully'. She posited that had she been a boy, her report might well have read 'A born leader'. So with taking. When boys and men take for themselves they are ambitious, when girls and women take for themselves we are grasping and selfish. But here, the man Jesus lets us know that he is there to be taken from. So the story may be said to offer us pictures of womanhood and manhood, which cut across our stereotypes and our gender constructions. So, like when Jesus and the woman, in reaching out, cut across taboos and brought about healing, we can say that in another way the same thing can happen. For as the story challenges stereotypical masculinity and femininity it may have the potential to liberate those men and women, who feel 'boxed in' by cultural constructions of what masculinity and femininity are supposed to be.

But more significant than this I think is the alternative picture of God which can be constructed from this story. Not the cruel God who heals or withholds healing according to his assessment of one's faith. Not the all-powerful, all-knowing God. Rather a picture more like the Good Friday God in Christ, to whom things happen over which he had no control. God who is not in control. People have a fear of not being in control. The worst human experiences we have are those where we feel out of control. Our bodies go wrong and we feel powerless to put them right. Our lives go wrong and we feel powerless to put them right. I think this story may speak to such situations, not calling for faith in a miracle we know can't happen, but in a way which can empower us to have faith in ourselves as the key to our wholeness. To begin with it may speak to an individual for whom things have gone wrong and who feels out of control, of a God who identifies with that out-of-controlness, and who at the point of our need connects with us. It speaks of a God who is there to be taken from, and whose grace is free. For as we take something of Godself into ourselves we may raise ourselves up into new life. Like the cycle of menstruation, with its phases of shedding and renewing, as we take from God the grace freely offered, we constantly open up for ourselves possibilities of becoming more fully human. It may also speak to the Christian community pastorally. For someone whose life has gone wrong may, like the woman, need to be able to take from others freely, without feeling guilty, may need to know that they are not taboo. At this point, we realize that our health or wholeness is not purely an individual matter, but that those around us significantly influence our capacity and our will to wholeness; in fact they have the potential to carry the resurrection hope for those who feel the rest of life is going to be one long Good Friday.

And so I put this reading back, but take this much away with me: That the woman who had no control over her illness connected with the God who had no control over God's power precisely at the point where she had enough faith in herself to reach out and take what she needed, not only for her own healing, but for the healing of her community. And so may her action be for us a model of healing. Amen.

Hazel Addy

RAHAB THE PROSTITUTE

Joshua 2; 6.17–25; (Luke 7.36–50); John 3.25–30

The New Testament reading originally chosen was the passage about a woman breaking the costly jar of ointment for Jesus as a token of his coming burial. The Gospel narratives are somewhat in disarray as to that lady's identity. But it was the hint of X Certificate in Luke's version 'a sinner from the city' which edified Victorians, and excited pre-Raphaelite visual imagination, which set my thoughts in a certain direction.

I felt nudged toward a particular line on Rahab, – one which I didn't want to take – what I might call the 'fallen woman makes good line' (to use that quaint phrase in the conventional sense which distinguishes some fallen women from the rest of us). For there is no suggestion in any part of our story that anyone is remotely interested in Rahab's sexual mores. It may indeed be that in the milieu in which the story originated 'Rahab the Prostitute' could be said as matter of factly as 'Rahab the Postmistress'. I was at first tempted, as I struggled for something to say about the woman, to give an address on Old Testament and Middle Eastern attitudes to sexuality: to remind you of how the prostitute in 'Never on a Sunday', played by Melina Mercouri, is the film's most free and generous human being, and to let you hear, or hear again Julian of Norwich.

> For I saw full assuredly that our substance is in God, and also I saw that in our sensualite God is: for in the self point that our Soul is made sensual, in the self point is the City of God ordained to Him from without beginning: into which seat he cometh and never shall remove it ...
>
> and as anent our substance and sensualite, it may rightly be cleped our soul: and that is because of the oneing that they have in God. The worshipful city that our Lord Jesus sitteth in is our sensualite in which He is enclosed: and our kindly substance is enclosed in Jesus with the blessed Soul of Christ sitting in rest in the Godhead.

However, exegetical honesty forces me to admit that it would be cheating to peg on this story any inferences about biblical attitudes to sex. There are none here. Rahab's profession may simply have been mentioned to identify a family whose Canaanite name stood out oddly in a later Israelite community, and needed explaining. Or it may be part of the story's motif to suggest in the by-going how two strangers could turn up without immediate ejection in any house within a town so on the defensive as Jericho. Indeed I have it on one authority (which sides with at least some commentators) that the Hebrew word used may simply mean hotel-keeper, and that even if the two offices sometimes, in the world's experience, coincide, there *need* be no innuendo in the word for Rahab's job, and none in the phrase 'they lodged with her': though it can mean what schoolboys of a certain age will take it to mean.

At any rate, there is not a scrap of moral comment around, whatever the lady's profession. Perhaps had she been a Canaanite temple-prostitute she would have provoked the raising of a negative editorial eyebrow (for we are dealing here with a story rehandled several hundred years after its origin) but nothing grounds that speculation either. Rahab's prostitution, whatever it was, refuses to be more than a casual matter of fact.

But whatever the lady's sex life there would be more grievous reasons for taking her as a bad lot. As the commentator J. Alberto Soggin nicely points out:

She receives the spies knowing who they are, hides them and collaborates closely with them, helps them escape, compromises herself irremediably over-against her fellow citizens. These services considerably exceed those which one normally expects from a prostitute.

Services they may be from Joshua's point of view, but from Jericho's they present the sort of barefaced treachery which takes the moral breath away, a kind of political act of treachery which would make any self-respecting partisan blench. No motivation is suggested which ameliorates her action. Terror, self-interested capitulation, and theological opportunism look suspiciously likely.

But again, not a whiff of moral indignation escapes from the narrative. *We* have to import it from our at least theoretical standards of patriotism and political integrity. This Deuteronomic account is the sort of cowboy story where the only good Canaanites are dead ones, and nothing so trivial as an individual's political dirty-handedness troubles the writer, provided God's people (and we all know which lot they are!) come out on top.

Let me then go back to the story of this story and set it. Its core is probably a kind of folk-legend going right back to the second millennium BC and told in the context of the shrine at Gilgal, part of the territory which emerged as Benjamite at the end of what we call 'The Exodus'. How much that Exodus was a slow patchy infiltration, with the Canaanites waking up too late to the fact, and how far it was a streamlined military campaign is much debated these days. But from what is certainly a streamlined narrative of pitched battles and toppling kings, one can pick out clues, dug out with the delicacy of literary archaeology, which support the infiltration idea.

This story may be one of these clues; at least it suggests the realism of an espionage network undertaking risky operations, a venture oddly redundant according to the main-line narrative whereby God predictably knocks the walls down to a trumpet-blast a few days later.

At any rate, the original story is probably the racy narrative about the concealment of the spies and the bargain struck with them which exempted Rahab and her house from the subsequent massacre.

But the really interesting thing about Rahab is what becomes of her, not in the personal but in the literary sense. Somewhere early in the seventh century and again in the sixth after the exile, person or persons unknown saw in this little local story from the Gilgal shrine a way of furthering his/their theological concerns. These concerns, commonly identified by the label Deuteronomic, emerged in the period after the great classical prophets who had challenged Israel to recognize a dangerous theological complacency and economic corruption, and had interpreted likely political events as divine judgment. Far from confident now, with Jerusalem sacked and the stresses of life in exile shaking their jejune piety to the core, the community was struggling against pressures towards disintegration and assimilation. In this context, the theological need seems, to the Deuteronomic school, to be consolidation not criticism. The distinctive unity of God's people under God's potent guidance was to be emphasized at all costs. The insignificance of pagan power against the purposes of Yahweh was to be rubbed in, and the hope of miraculous success against humanly insuperable odds to be rekindled.

So the little Rahab story is expanded and the narrative filled out with great emphasis on the psychological collapse of the Canaanites in the face of Israel's God and his representatives (though it slips out in the course of Joshua 26, where the lines get a little crossed, that the men of Jericho put up a fight).

Above all, Rahab is made a paradigm of instant and total conversion to Israelite monotheistic faith, uttering words which, as Wellhausen suggested, have a ring about them 'as if she had read the entire Pentateuch' whose existence lay centuries ahead of hers.

The Deuteronomic editor, so to speak, takes his theological pleasure of Rahab, as do nearly all subsequent commentators until the scrupulous historical-analytical exegetes of the last hundred years or so, who have hardly, perhaps, much concept of theological pleasure. But before that, Rahab had an extraordinary amount of theological manhandling. To the Jews she was a prototype of proselyte baptism from among the Gentiles; for some early fathers a figure of the Gentile church. To the writer

of Hebrews she is a paradigmatic heroine of faith. For the author
of James a signal example of justification by works. For Clement
of Alexandria she prefigures with her scarlet rope the need of
atonement 'showing that by the blood of our Lord should be
redemption to all that believe and hope in God'. For Calvin
she illustrates God's dynamic vocation to join the elect. For
Edmund Leach of structural anthropology she is with structural
appropriateness to be identified with Rechab, the ancestral
foundress of the Rechabites (a point which the Professor of
Hebrew would be happy to have me point out can only appear to
stand, because English versions of scripture don't all reproduce
the difference between two Hebrew consonants!).

The real historical Rahab, where is she in all this? Does she
undergo in her interpreting a more subtle and sinister mode of
prostitution, becoming all sorts of theological things to all men.

Or does her story illustrate something of the legitimate freedom
of faith that can so play with the past?

Certainly it was manifestly assumed as a freedom in the early
Christian church: and I chose the Fourth Gospel passage about
John the Baptist to offer a New Testament parallel to the Rahab
story-process. Almost certainly the historical John the baptizer
made no such speech. Almost certainly the writer of the Gospel
didn't care twopence that he didn't. His purpose was to exalt
Jesus, and existing traditions would be better grist to his theological mill with a bit of editorial enlargement. So what that it
never happened quite like that! Theologically it ought to have
done.

Now we live in a world which is intellectually more squeamish
about conflating history and imagination. We are afraid of
prostituting the intact past by forcing documentary fact to yield
to our theological seductions. We regard the fruit of such unions
as illegitimate.

The church father Origen in the first half of the third century
was more intellectually abandoned. In his homily on Leviticus he
writes:

> You must be prepared to recognize that the narratives of Holy
> scripture are figures and for that reason you must consider
> them in a spiritual rather than a carnal fashion, and thus grasp

their purport. For if you take them in a carnal manner they harm you and fail to nourish.

What's prostitution then, or carnal reading? What's spiritual flexibility? Let me close, again with Origen, this time on John.

I do not condemn the Evangelists even if they sometimes modified things which in the eye of history happened differently, in the interests of the mystical aim which they had in view: so that they speak of a thing which happened in one place as if it happened somewhere else, or of what took place at one time as if it had happened at another time, and introduce certain changes into the words actually spoken. Their intention was to speak the truth, when it is possible, both materially and spiritually, and when it was not possible to do both, they preferred the spiritual to the material. Indeed spiritual truth was often preserved in what might be described as material falsehood.

How's that for a last word on the meaning of Rahab the Prostitute?

Elizabeth Templeton

THE MASSACRE OF THE INNOCENTS

Matthew 2.1–18

Think back to the Christmas cards you received this year. How many of you had cards with a picture of Father Christmas? How many cards had a picture of the wise men? And how many had a picture of the Massacre of the children? I have never received a card remembering the Massacre – not in all my life. And, I don't think it appears in the traditional nine lessons and carols. Why? Because we want to keep Christmas nice? Because the story is too awful to be told? The shepherds and wise men appear in our Christmas cribs, along with angels and stars and sheep and cows and donkeys, but no bloodied babies, no slaughtered toddlers. The massacred innocents do not appear in the cut-out paste nativity scenes or the knitting patterns. And it has always been like this – the forgotten Christmas story.

But this year (1992), around Christmas time, it seems almost more than any other year, we have been faced with our own terrible stories about children. If Christmas means anything at all, if what we have celebrated is something that can truly give hope and meaning to our lives, then we must be able to hold that story alongside our own stories, even our stories of suffering and terror, and know that God has spoken to us. What can we say when we hear of children going hungry in Somalia, of children caught in crossfire in Somalia. What can we say when we hear of fourteen-year old Benji Stanley shot as he queued for food in a Moss Side takeaway? What can we say when we hear of Suzanne from Moston burnt beyond recognition, tortured and left to die on a Stockport golfcourse? What can we say when we know that children in Ordsall are offered transfers to place on their hands and when you lick them off they taste nice because they have LSD in them? All around us innocents are still facing death and children are losing their innocence too young.

For us, as for all people, a religion that is merely sentiment and that refuses to face the terror of living will not do. Sometimes we may be tempted to see our faith as the place where everything horrible is cut out and where we forget for a moment the shades and the pain. But in a faith of forgetting, true joy and hope will also be lost. It's true isn't it – that it's the people who have faced the most suffering who are often the people who have real hope. When we have faced the depths, we know what it is to grasp for deliverance.

Today is the first Sunday after Epiphany. At Epiphany we think about the wise men and their stupendous gifts. But today, we must think of the slaughtered children. For the sake of the mother of Benji, of the mother of Suzanne, for the sake of the children of Somalia and of Bosnia, we must remember the story of the slaughtered children and seek there to find understanding of the world's sorrow and to reach out for true hope.

It's funny, but I suppose understandable, that we usually separate the story of the wise men (three kings) from the horrifying story of the slaughter. We speak of them as though they were two separate events. We might remember vaguely that Herod got the idea that there was a new king coming from the wise men, but we are still able to celebrate the wise men without remembering the terrible consequence of their foolishness. Some years I have been to a service in the cathedral – held on this Sunday after Epiphany – a grand and splendid service of celebration. There are people dressed in fine and elegant robes – kings and pages. They process round the cathedral to beautful music and present their glamorous gifts upon the altar. It is a fine experience full of grandeur and elegance, but there is no mention of the slaughter – that would be incongruous – just like the ragged tramps who wait outside for the smart worshippers to come out. But the story of wise men is also the story of the slaughter. In the Bible, it is one story, not two. And I suppose that many people would recognize that in their own experience. Benji's mother knows that her son's death is tied up with the sophisticated battles of the drug barons – the mothers of Somalia know that their children die because of the wisdom of the clan leaders who keep the civil war going. The mothers of Bosnia know that their children die because of the disputes of powerful men. Wherever the powerful struggle with one another, the innocent die. And I am sure that in Bethlehem too, mothers know this secret. In my imagination I can hear such a mother speaking out to the wise men. Their story is often told. Let us hear hers.

The day does not belong to me and you are not my kind. I will never be famous like you. My voice will not be heard, only my weeping will find its way into history. From me there will be no act of devotion, only protest and pleading and pain. I live in the nameless realm where women live. I have no name and no voice, only tears. I will never be there in the nursery firelight, in the picture books and the toys, for my story is too hard to bear. This day does not belong to me, and the future will be yours. I will live forever in the nameless realm, but you will be feted by the faithful and named fantastically; Caspar, Melchior, Balthazar. I have no name, but that of woman.

You were late in coming, they say. A cold coming, they say. I wish you had never come at all. Because of your foolishness, my sons lie cold in my arms and their time is over. With the other women, I weep bitter tears and my heart is broken. Nathan was almost two and he was so funny; into everything, asking 'Why?' all the time, like they do. He was talking quite well, with just a faint lisp. He was a good child, but he was lively, very bright and we all thought he would make something of himself one day. He had just learnt to say a prayer and his father had thought ... well, it doesn't matter now. He won't be saying any more prayers. And Joshua, just a tiny baby, only three weeks old. He was small, but I was sure that he would live. I had just got him feeding well, and I was beginning even to enjoy those night feeds; just the two of us together in the silent night while the world slept – and we were there nursing in the night, lit only by the stars. And now my breasts are full and painful. My body does not yet know that my sons are dead, though their blood is dry on my skin. I wonder if you have children. Did you leave them behind to come here and visit someone else's child? Now, perhaps you will go back and your children will be there to greet you, holding out chubby arms to welcome you home. But my children are dead.

The soldiers came just as I had finished giving Joshua the early morning feed and Nathan was just waking. I thought they had come for my husband and I stood up to tell them that he had already left for work. Then one of them grabbed Nathan. I almost thought for a moment that he wanted to play with him; he put his arm round Nathan's neck from behind like men do sometimes when they play with boys. And then he slit his throat. And how can I bear even to remember it? Nathan's outraged eyes, his red, red blood, his ending and mine. And I gave them Joshua. He was tiny in their hands and the knife was bigger than he was. And I gave them Joshua. And they killed him. I could hear screams, but they weren't mine. I could hear Mary next door and Naomi. And I could hear the little boy over the way who was stubborn in dying. And I could hear my own heart beat and the sound of blood dripping on the floor. You were late in coming. I wish you had never come at all.

They say you came carefully, calculating everything and working it all out, planning the route and what you would say and what you would bring. Well, you didn't work it out well enough. You blundered severely. They call you wise men, but any fool could have seen what would happen. Did you really think that Herod would be pleased to know he had a rival? Did you really expect a great king to be pleased to know what you knew? Foolish, silly men. And what gifts you brought. Did you really think that it was sensible to bring gold into a district like this? Do you really not yet understand the ways of God, whose ways are not the ways of men? And I do not find your foolishness charming or amusing, for it cost me my children.

You stopped to call on Herod to exchange compliments. Didn't you realize that it does no good to pay compliments to tyrants, that you were wasting your time and risking our lives? I do not forgive your naivety or think you innocent. You are men of the world, and yet the women in the markets know better than you the danger that lurks in a king's parlour. The blood of our sons is on your hands. You are not my kind. You wanted compliments too, I suppose. You wanted to rest in a king's palace after your long, cold journey. You wanted women and sherbert and flattering words. And I have no flattering words for you, foolish men. The innocent have suffered and the guilt is yours.

You are not my patrons. You cannot be the patrons of any mother who cares for her sons. You were confused by your own snobbery and stupidity, your own blindness to the world's way. And yet history calls you wise and does not even let me speak. Only my weeping is heard, my sobbing in bitter grief that refuses to be comforted. I will hear no excuses from you or from your God. And my tears are more eloquent than your wisdom. Do not pray for me, for I refuse even the comforts of God.

How can we respond to a mother's cry and to the cry of all mothers and fathers? Does it look to them as though God in the Bible story escaped the pain of the slaughter? The Jesus child has all the luck of the gods and leaves behind the real suffering, fleeing into Egypt. Did Mary ever look back on the suffering town and feel guilty that her son had escaped the killing? And did she think of that moment as she held the body of her son on calvary, as they lifted him down from the cross? Our faith tells us that God does not escape the pain – that God is as close as our own breathing with those who suffer.

Our faith celebrates the coming of God among us in Jesus. And that we know at Christmas. Our faith also affirms that God suffers with us, that God in Jesus has faced the terror of death and given us hope in its face. And so I want to ask, Could not our salvation have been wrought if Jesus had died with the innocents – if God had truly embraced human living and dying here? For I find God in the weeping women who refused to be comforted and in the children who were slaughtered without mercy. And I believe that in the tears of Rachel's weeping can be heard the sound of God. And in that sound is a source of true hope, the hope that those who suffer truly know. We do have something to say to Benji's mother and to Suzanne's mother and to all those who have faced life at its bitterest. God is with us. God is with us.

Jesus was born at Bethlehem. After the birth, three wise women from the East arrived. They asked quietly among the midwives where the child was and found him quickly. They brought with them gifts for the child; a clean linen gown, some oil for his skin and some fragrance for his bath. They embraced Mary, the child's mother, and they talked of giving birth and shared the secrets of women. They cuddled the child and smiled into his eyes and wept with joy to see God in the face of a baby. Then, a great silence fell over the land and there was terror in the hearts of the people. The silence was broken by the sounds of crying and the slaughter began. No one knew why the soldiers came so late at night, or why they killed the babies. What reason could they have had? And who had time to search for reasons, or the strength to ask the philosophers' questions? There was only room for weeping and for grief. And they came for Mary's child and killed him, piercing his body with a spear. Mary wept for her child. The wise women embraced her, but she would not be comforted. And a voice was heard in Rama, sobbing in bitter grief; it was God weeping for her children, refusing to be comforted.

Susan Durber

CROSSING THE BORDER

Matthew 15.21–31

The rabbi is tired. He is tired of communicating with people who listen only for an opportunity to twist his words. He is worn out with loving them, and drained by the effort of sharing a vision that is always refused. He wants to go away, and leave their squabbles far behind. He wants to hide from malicious eyes and pointing fingers. He will not say, but he also seeks escape from the clumsy, uncomprehending love of his friends.

The rabbi longs to take his pain to the solitude of the hills. There he will find peace, and renew his strength. But his friends will not let him go:

'You must not travel alone – the road is dangerous and you have made powerful enemies with your talk. It's too big a risk.'

Sensing their anxiety, the rabbi relents:

'Yes, you may come with me ... we'll rest over the border for a few weeks. No one will point us out abroad.'

So the hope of solitude is lost for the sake of those who love him, yet once again fail to grasp his need.

Still a foreign country offers freedom of a kind. He will find freedom on the busy road to the sea, where a band of foreigners is worth no more than a passing glance. He will find freedom in the great cities of the coast, where tall ships bring people of all nations to live together in haughty indifference. He will not find the longed-for solitude, but at least a temporary release from his people's demands.

So the rabbi and his companions are leaving the lake, the gossip of the market-place, the scandals denounced in the synagogues, and the arguments that rage in every household. Eyes watch as they climb the road that leads through the fishing villages, towards the hills and the border beyond:

'We've seen his kind before. They promise the world, but our ways are not so easily changed.'

They have taught the rabbi a lesson, and are confident that he will not come back to Galilee. Some say so with satisfaction, but others watch him go with a sadness they scarcely understand.

The woman has hidden for two days in the shadow of the rock. The water-gourd is nearly empty, and the remains of the bread are stale and hard. It is hot, though the nights are cold. For two days she has been waiting, her eyes fixed on the road.

She never meant to stay out so long, or to brave the night terrors of the hills. She never meant to abandon her family, or thought she could ever leave her daughter behind. She never meant to risk her reputation for a rumour ... Yet she will break all rules for the sake of a hope she has nursed since the birth of her first child.

Others gave up hope long ago. The women of the village, gentle with the baby, are embarrassed by the child. They are impatient with her longing for a cure:

'You can do nothing for the girl, so let her be. Life carries on ... Think of your husband, your fine, strong sons, and be thankful.'

The woman does think of her husband. She thinks of her fine, strong sons, and is truly thankful. But she cannot forget her dark-eyed, angry child.

For thirteen years the woman has loved her wild daughter with a love both fierce and tender. She has learned to fear for her child, and now she fears more than the casual cruelties of children in the market. She is afraid because the girl is becoming a woman, and she watches the look in young men's eyes with growing dread. The woman-child is beautiful, but none of those who stand and stare will ask to be her husband. She dare not abandon her daughter to their protection, or entrust her to the care of the young men's gods.

Only hope can secure a future for her child. The woman's hope is urgent now, but will not be deceived. It has tested the claims of countless faith-healers and quacks. It has taught her to mistrust hands that withhold healing as they reach out for gold. It has taught her to discern the lies on men's lips, and yet to keep listening for the note of truth in their words. Now, after thirteen years, she knows that note has sounded.

Rumours have travelled from across the border. Tales of a young rabbi are carried by sailors returning to their ships, pedlars passing through the village, and beggars kicked from door to door. The people this man heals are sworn to silence, and he does not ask for gold. Yet the rabbi has angered the holy men, and they say he is forced to travel abroad. Two days ago a traveller claimed to have passed him on the way to Tyre from Galilee. He must pass through their land.

So the woman waits in the shadow of the rock. Her eyes are fixed on the road. This time her hope will not be refused.

The disciple is angry with the rabbi, and will not join the others by the fire after the evening meal. Why did the rabbi act as he did? He feels let down, and afraid.

It happened towards the end of a long day's walk. Only a mile to the next resting place, and they were passing a rock at the side of the road. Suddenly there was a scream, a scarcely human sound. The disciple was frightened. It might have been an animal, or one of the robber bands that prey upon travellers at dusk. But once the disturbance was over, he could see only a woman of the land.

Everyone looked to the rabbi, but he looked straight ahead as if he had not heard. Then he said something about the lost sheep of Israel. It seemed a strange reply, for surely the woman was only a beggar in search of food. The travellers moved on without another word. But the woman wouldn't stop shouting, and began to follow them down the road. Then the disciple began to plead with the rabbi:

'Give her something – anything – just get her off our backs.'

In the end the woman forced the issue, by running ahead and throwing herself across the track. Now the disciple could see her properly, even though the light had almost disappeared. Despite the dust on her clothing, she looked strangely respectable and not the kind to beg at the side of the road.

The woman spoke directly to the rabbi. The disciple cannot remember exactly what she said. Yet, as she spoke, he began to realize what this woman wanted. He hadn't really listened before, conscious only of noise and not words. She didn't want money, or a charm against evil. She actually wanted the rabbi himself. She wanted to drain him with her need as others had in Galilee. But this woman could have no claim on the rabbi. Hadn't he told them to go only among their own people, who alone would share in the promises of God?

The disciple still cannot believe what the rabbi did. He spoke directly to the woman, calling her by the name they all had for foreigners. 'Little dog', he called her, though gently enough. The reproof should have been final. But the woman caught the rabbi's words almost before they fell. She answered back. It was unthinkable . . . a foreign woman dared to better the rabbi. Yet worse was to come, for her wish was granted. She had changed his mind.

So the disciple's world is turned upsidedown by an act of insolence which the rabbi calls faith. He has been taught not to mix with foreigners, and knows that the anger of the prophets is fiercest against those who desert a jealous God. He is proud to stand apart, and know himself chosen and special. The disciple has delighted in his calling since boyhood. Yet this no longer matters to the rabbi.

The disciple is afraid. The border has been breached, and now any one who comes will expect a share of his reward. He does not know where the story of the woman's victory will end.

So where does the story end? For the woman? For the rabbi? For the disciple and all who long to share in the promises of God?

I do not know what happened to the woman after her wish was granted. I would like to follow her back to the village, and to tell of that first meeting with her daughter. I would like to imagine the lives they were able to lead. But the Gospel writer does not say, and I am left with the memory of one woman's hope for her child. Yet memory is powerful. I cannot forget the audacity of her hope. I cannot forget the persistence that accepts no refusal, and the courage that dares to answer back. I cannot forget that this woman's hope, persistence and courage had power to change the mind of God.

For the rabbi did return to Galilee. He returned as he had come, back along the road that leads through the hills and down to the lake. Once again crowds began to gather, only this time they were different from before. There were people of many races, languages and religions, and the rabbi moved among them all. He made no distinctions, seeing only human beings in their sickness and need. He reached out, and many were healed. The promise once wrested from him by a foreign woman was now shared freely with the crowd.

But what of the disciple? He returned with the rabbi and watched the crowds gather as they had before. He saw the dumb speak, the maimed made whole, the lame walk, and sight restored to the eyes of the blind. He saw a child run into the open arms of the rabbi. He heard many tongues sing out for joy to his God. Then he no longer felt as if he had been robbed. The promises were still his, but now the disciple knew that they were not for him to guard. His fear fell away, and he began to understand. The borders of God's promise were open, and would never again be closed.

Alison Peacock

4

Speaking for Ourselves

As he waits for the service to begin, the male preacher may wait in a vestry lined with photo-portraits of other men who have shared this pulpit and he will feel at home. He will read Bible accounts of male heroes and will tell inspiring stories of the founding fathers; from Abraham to Wesley, from Moses to Calvin, from Jesus to Romero. He will, for the most part, make his God in the image of these male figures and will sense with pride his own belonging to all of this. The male preacher has a rich stock of history and heroes from which to draw. But, the preacher who is a woman does not stand in the same relation to the history of her forebears as her male colleague.

The heroes and historical traditions of the Christian faith have been predominantly male or androcentric. In any list of saints and saints' days, there are more men to be remembered than women and the women who are there are often remembered for 'virtues' associated with patriarchal ideals of holy womanhood. The records of the faith have been kept by men and in male interests. In the words of the hymn, 'We come unto our fathers' God'. Consequently, much Christian preaching has been about the retelling of the traditions for today, the faithful carrying on of the story and the naming of the heroes. The woman preacher cannot place herself unproblematically within this tradition and neither can she accept without protest the way in which the stories of the women have been silenced and the women heroes forgotten. Women are no longer accepting the role and status ascribed to them by patriarchy. As Daphne Hampson claims, 'Women are conjuring up a new sense of themselves'. This new sense is beginning to find a voice in the pulpit, where women who preach are 'speaking for ourselves' and refusing to speak for the androcentric traditions.

Many feminist theologians and preachers are working hard to

uncover lost or hidden traditions, 'searching for lost coins' in the dust of patriarchy. The assumption is that there have always been good and strong women amongst our forebears, but that their stories have been left untold or have been silenced. Feminist research has regained some of these lost histories and lost themes.

> The good news is that great women have always walked the earth ... their footprints are still clear ... their presence has changed things both in church and society. (Chittister, 1990; p. 28)

New resources for the preaching of women (and of men) have come to light as the footprints of the women of the tradition have been unearthed. Women have discovered that we can speak for ourselves from the pulpit, naming our own history in our own way. We have recognized the patriarchalization of the tradition and have developed strategies to unfold alternative histories and heroes. Sometimes there is little to go on – a name with no history at the end of a Pauline letter, a woman's story told only from an androcentric perspective, long silences in the recorded history of a patriarchal church, folk stories and legends, memories passed on from mother to daughter or shared at women's gatherings. But sometimes we sense that the treasure is rich and plentiful and that at last we are beginning to claim the abundance which is rightfully ours. In speaking for ourselves, we thirst for the deep well-springs of God and our thirst will not go unquenched.

Feminist biblical scholars have worked to unearth lost stories and traditions in the biblical texts. For example, Elisabeth Schüssler Fiorenza has argued that the first Christian communities were egalitarian and that women originally held strong positions of leadership. Patriarchal culture quickly swallowed up these noble beginnings, but traces of that early history and of the women who took their place within it remain within the text; Phoebe, Priscilla and Junia, for example, who were women leaders of the early church. The presence of their names bears witness to a lost history and to lost voices which we can now reclaim as ours.

Similarly, women can draw on the story of Mary Magdalene, the first witness of the resurrection and apostle to the apostles, as a powerful testimony to the trust which God has given to women to bear the good news for all people. The story of the male disciples who refused to believe her also has strong parallels with women's experience of the church. Women have discovered the power of such accounts and of many others to name our present experience and to bring hope and affirmation into our fear and frustration. An example of such claiming of our own biblical heritage and narrative, as well as later history, is *A Litany of Women's Power*, written by Ann M. Heidkamp and published in a resource book for the WCC Decade of Churches in Solidarity with Women. The litany names the power of Sarah's faith, the courage of Esther and Deborah, the belief of Mary Magdalene and the other women who followed Jesus, and the power of Phoebe and Priscilla to spread the gospel and to inspire congregations. As the litany ends, all are invited to say,

> We have celebrated the power of many women past and present. It is time now to celebrate ourselves. Within each of us is that same life and light and love. Within each of us lie the seeds of power and glory. Our bodies can touch with love; our hearts can heal; our minds can seek out faith and truth and justice. Spirit of Life, be with us in our quest. Amen. (WCC Publications, 1988; p. 72)

Rich resources have also been discovered in the history of the church beyond and since the writing of the biblical texts. There have been many notable women in the life of the church who have written theology, preached the gospel, nourished faith and spirituality and worked to change society. More and more, their stories are being told and becoming a renewed resource for the life of the whole church and particularly for women. While it remains true that church history has been dominated by men, there is an alternative history which women can claim as their own. We have discovered the rich treasures to be found in the stories of such mediaeval women mystics and theologians as Hildegard of Bingen, Julian of Norwich, Mechtild of Magdeburg, Catherine of Siena and Margery Kempe. We have drawn inspiration from women like Anne Askew, a woman who died in the sixteenth century for the right to interpret the Bible for herself, and from Elizabeth Cady Stanton who produced *The Woman's Bible* in 1895 and who also campaigned tirelessly against slavery.

We have drawn courage and hope from the stories of the tenacity of women preachers from nonconformist traditions in the eighteenth and early nineteenth centuries, who preached the gospel despite opposition because of their gender. Nicola Slee comments in her sermon on Hildegard of Bingen, included in this section:

> It is a terrible tragedy and injustice that Hildegard's voice, along with so many other wise and gifted voices of women, has been forgotten for all these centuries of Western history.

The depth of the tragedy should not be underestimated. Women are justly angry that a great injustice has been committed against us and still remains. Now we are seizing opportunities to reclaim what we can of our story and to tell it with boldness. We do not have to tell the faith through the stories of great or humble Christian men, but we can speak for ourselves, from the resources of our past, from the depths of our imaginations and from our shared experiences as women today. We have our own story to tell and we will tell it.

In this reclaiming of our history, we are not looking for flawless models, but for our lost and silenced foremothers in the faith. In solidarity with them, with their struggle and pain, their power and their weakness too, we can find a source of wisdom and strength. We do not expect to find a pure and untainted tradition (none exists nor could exist), but a history of courageous women who spoke for themselves in their time and so can speak to us in ours. It may be that sometimes imagination and fantasy will replace for us what has been lost or destroyed from our women's story, but we will carefully preserve the traces that remain of those women who have walked before us.

In the past, women who were learning to be preachers had few role models. Unlike their male colleagues they did not have many 'heroes' of their own gender to encourage and empower them. To some extent, and for some women, this remains true today. But, because more and more women are finding a voice and because theology is beginning, in some cases, to find its shape within the context of women's experience and history, women are seizing the courage to 'speak for ourselves'. Hearing other women preach, experiencing the ministry of ordained women, discovering the hidden resources of women in the tradition and using our own experience and imagination in our theology has given us all bravery and affirmation. Though women still weep in the churches and are still silenced and abused, we are gaining courage from each other. As Carol M. Noren has written, in her book *The Woman in the Pulpit*,

> When a woman who is a role model testifies to the divine, enabling grace at work in her own life and ministry, her successors learn to claim its sustaining power for themselves. (Noren, 1991, p. 30)

The sermons in this section all bear witness to the renewed power of women who have begun to 'speak for ourselves'. In her sermon on Eve, Janet Lees shows how the story of a woman who has been an anti-hero for the tradition can become a source of liberation and encouragement for women who want to seek wisdom – we can tell the story our way. Ann Loades, in her sermon on Mary of Magdala, shows powerfully the significant place of Mary within the text as the first witness of the resurrection – one bearing apostolic authority. She challenges the church to place its confidence in women who believe themselves to be heirs of this tradition about Mary. Nicola Slee and Lavinia Byrne both give voice to some of the rich resources of women's theology and spiritual wisdom. Nicola Slee brings to her preaching the life and theology of Hildegard of Bingen and prays that it is not too late for such a voice as hers to be heard. Lavinia Byrne draws our attention to the lives of women, both past and present, famous and unknown, who have touched and strengthened the life of one faith community in London. In her gentle appeal she encourages us to remember and to honour the lives of such diverse, but all heroic, women. Janet Wootton's sermon is an historic one, preached at the outset of the WCC Decade of Churches in Solidarity with Women. Janet draws on biblical stories of heroic women leaders and also on the history of her own tradition, one of the first to recognize the ministry of women, to inspire her hearers. Bridget Rees gives us a very different picture of heroic women, women who have seized the courage to leave the church, to say 'enough is enough' and to go, like the people of Israel, into the wilderness. All these sermons, and many like them, bear eloquent testimony to the courage and strength of women – 'speaking for ourselves'.

————

BLAMING EVE

Genesis 3.1–13; I Timothy 2.8–15; John 4.5–42

At the beginning of the sermon a flip chart with the text I Tim. 2.12 'I permit no woman to teach or to have authority over a man; she is to keep silent' written on it and placed in full view of the congregation was followed by a period of silence. Then I took an apple from a bowl on the communion table, rubbed it on my chest and bit it.

Well, we could sit here in silence for the next twenty minutes, or we could risk it. The silence wouldn't do us any harm, but it's probably not what you're expecting. I admit to having eaten the apple, so I'll risk it.

I'm glad to say that the United Reformed Church is an equal opportunity employer, particularly with new resolutions about employment practice which were passed at General Assembly. Unfortunately, that doesn't immediately lead to the defeat of sexism in the church. One of the major resources used by both sides of the sexism debate is scripture. There are few more popular passages than the two from Genesis 3 and I Timothy 2. Equal opportunities or not, the battle of the sexes still rages in our churches. It's hardly surprising for it still rages in our society. We take action against racism, boycott apartheid, condemn genocide and racial harassment; all rightly so. But the evil that lies at the root of our social disease we fail to take seriously; that is the whole business by which women and men relate to each other.

The relationship between women and men is a fundamental part of life on this earth. This is echoed in the creation account of Genesis. There, right at the beginning of the scriptural record, after the awe-inspiring act of the creation of the whole cosmic order, the scene is set for the rest of history; and in human terms it specifically means that the relationship between women and men is broken.

[Take apples from bowl on Communion table and throw them to members of the congregation in the following bit]

We all know who ate the apple: Eve did. Eve did; a weak woman who wanted to be wise. Here, you're one, you're an Eve. And you, and you, and you and ... me ... Yes, me ..., I ate the apple ... I ate the apple ... I ate the apple ... Yes, I ATE THE APPLE.

[me as Eve, holding apple]

> I accept responsibility for eating the apple. I ate the apple. I wanted the knowledge. I wanted to become wise. I accept the responsibility for the knowledge. It wasn't all I thought it would be; there was knowledge of good things. There was also knowledge of bad things. There was knowledge of joy and happiness but also knowledge of pain and suffering. At first it wasn't easy to accept responsibility for all this knowledge. I wanted to blame someone else. I blamed the snake, saying I'd been tricked. It was easier to blame someone else than accept the responsibility myself. I wanted to hide from this new responsibility, this new wisdom. So I blamed someone else. But I did eat the apple. It is my responsibility. I cannot blame anyone else. The responsibility for the knowledge and the way the knowledge is used is mine. I ate the apple. I ATE THE APPLE!
>
> Of course Adam blamed me, but should I hold that against him? After all I blamed someone else too; I blamed the snake. It's not surprising; we didn't know how God would react, we were afraid. Adam blamed me because he didn't want the responsibility and I blamed the snake because I didn't want the responsibility either. As it is we both got more than we bargained for; we both got hard labour. More than that, in our blaming of each other we set up a stumbling block in our relationship. In our failure to accept responsibility we began to grow a mistrust of each other. The result of this is that we failed to share our labours as we had before. Each one was burdened with their own concerns. We drifted further apart. I found it hard to see his point of view and he failed to see mine. We were

continually blaming each other for the things that went wrong; when work went badly he'd blame me, when the children got sick I'd blame him, when the food was inedible we'd blame each other. The arguments always ended in the same way; I ate the apple. We failed to accept our individual and joint responsibilities and continued to blame each other.

[bite apple again and put it on communion table].

Unfortunately, this story of blaming someone else has continued on down the ages. The writer of I Timothy also had the tendency; it wasn't me, it was her.

The problem that this writer was addressing is also relevant to us; how should we worship God. Unfortunately he (more likely than she, I suspect) got sidetracked by the old chestnut: 'who blames who'. It is clear that in this situation, where Christianity was just taking hold and orthodoxy was being established, a lot of other influences were going around in the churches. The manner and style of prayer, the mode of dress and the ministry of women, where issues that required consideration in the ordering of church life. The writer seems to have been concerned about where to draw the line in terms of the type and style of worship that should be offered. Some things might be disruptive. The philosophical view of a split between nature and spirit which had men as spiritual and women as natural or earthy lead to the construction of the view that what women did was unsuitable for worship. This had to be rationalized through the use of the scriptural record and so the writer of I Timothy continued to blame Eve.

One of the effects of the movement to regularize church worship was the way in which the contribution of women was marginalized. They became the passive recipients of worship which was lead by men. This was not just bad for women, as, for example, a factor in reinforcing the door-mat tendency. It was also bad for men, who always had to learn how to lead in a dominant way. It lead to several centuries of sexual separatism in church worship. Whilst not actually relegating women to worship in separate places to men, it meant that their opportunities to share gifts and ministries was diminished. The modern church has also inherited these problems in the 'to ordain or not to ordain' women debate and the 'why are there fewer men in the pews' dilemma. But of course that's not relevant to the right on equal opportunities URC, is it?

Whilst the specific discussion about the call of women to leadership and teaching roles within our denomination might be moving down the road towards equality, the essential debate about who takes responsibility in church life and worship, both in the local situation and nationally continues to be pertinent. We have opened up the structures to some extent, but the deep rooted nature of sexism means that our ability to really share, work co-operatively, recognize and value each others contributions without being patronizing continue to require attention in both our individual and communal lives.

So how can we achieve this? Will we ever get the balance right? We seem to need someone to show us the way, someone who will struggle with these problems and show us God's way of doing things. Someone who knows God's way so well that there is a unity between them and God, so the plan of action is integrated and whole. But also someone who knows us well, knows what it's like to be us and struggle with our problems. Enter Jesus.

Jesus seems to do it all rather differently. The rules are the rules and the law is the law, but in the scene from John chapter 4, Jesus is once again pointing out so many limitations of the old ways. Jews and Samaritans or women and men; either way they weren't supposed to mix like this. But Jesus seems to be prepared to start new kinds of relationships which transcend the old human barriers.

One of the things Jesus asks for in these new relationships is honesty. We can't go on blaming each other for the breaking down of our relationships or the stumbling blocks. When Jesus asks the questions, like the woman in the story, we find out that we are compelled to give honest answers. She'd had a number of previous husbands and the status of her present relationship is not clear. Jesus does not condemn her for any of this, but he does ask her to be honest about it and face up to the responsibility. So with us, the message is not so much that there are a set rules which determine the number or the status of our relationships, but rather that the first stage in making these right relationships requires honesty.

If we don't get on with someone, find them hard to work with or live with, the first stage in healing the relationship has to be honesty. If the relationships we have and the commitments that come with them, make it difficulties in other areas of our life, such that we become too busy for all our commitments, then the first step to take in making it right is to be honest. Not easy. It's quite likely to hurt before things move on to a better balance. But we have to bear our part of the responsibility before we can expect to make progress in restoring the relationship.

Having moved away from the tendency to blame each other or hide from the reality of the situation and the responsibility that brings; in other words having come clean, we are ready to move on into a new relationship. As forgiven people we can sart again with God and with others. This new relationship is what lies at the heart of our Christian calling. It is a relationship in which women and men do not have to resort to blaming each other but can value each other's contributions as they seek to work together.

So as we wait now, whether in Jerusalem or some other place, for the coming of the Holy Spirit, which is the promise of Pentecost, let's prepare ourselves. It's an opportunity to take stock of our relationships, to make another move towards each other in reconciliation, admitting our responsibilities as honestly as we can. If we begin to do this and let our relationships be made new by God's Spirit then we will be ready to respond to Jesus' call to worship God in spirit and in truth.

Janet Lees

MARY OF MAGDALA*

John 20.11–18

The reading from John's Gospel connects together themes of death and life, losing and finding, absence and presence, all characteristic of the time in the liturgical year when Christians rehearse the death, resurrection-ascension, and then spirit-giving

---

* A sermon given at King's College, Cambridge on 24 May 1992.

of their saviour. As is happens, we also anticipate by only a day, the feast day of the three Mary's-Mary of Magdala, Mary the wife of Cleophas, and Mary the mother of James, all associated with the scenes of the death and burial of Christ, and Mary of Magdala in particular with the resurrection stories. And beyond that day, we anticipate the feast of the ascension this coming Thursday.

I want to focus on one Mary, Mary of Magdala, not only because of her centrality in the Gospel text, but also because attention to her vividly illustrates the way in which even very familiar Gospel texts can still come alive for us, make a point for us. The novelists Nikos Kazantzakis, Michelle Roberts and Rudyard Kipling as well as the poet HD in her work 'The Flowering of the Rod' have all written about her in this century, direct heirs of a long tradition beyond the canonical Gospels which has made Mary of Magdala both so attractive and so problematic. What are we in our turn to make of this patron saint of those who make cosmetics and perfume, of hairdressing and the adornment of the body, the evangelist of southern France, where her relics provoked some tough competition between mediaeval monasteries eager to attract pilgrims to their shrines? Even if we stay within the limits of the Gospel texts, how many of these can we link together, after all the criticism of habits of interpretation in the Western church at any rate, which have associated one Mary with another, unnamed women with those who are named, and all these especially with Mary of Magdala identified so clearly in the Fourth Gospel as the first resurrection witness?

This fact alone might well prompt hearers of the Gospels, as these texts were shaped in the early years of telling and re-telling them, to hunt across the material for what would feed heart and imagination, make some sort of portrait of Mary, and so help understand the exchange between her and the one she mistook for the gardener. I'm not going to focus on the resurrection narratives themselves, odd enough in all conscience, except to say that this particular one isn't the only one to make a point of the way in which Christ wasn't always immediately recognized – think of the walk to Emmaus in Luke's Gospel. But it's worth especially recalling that strange story in Matthew's Gospel of Mary of Magdala and another Mary, running from the tomb,

meeting Christ, falling to their knees, and grabbing hold of his
feet – rather incapacitating for all concerned. That's what may lie
somewhere behind those almost untranslatable words, often
rendered as 'Don't touch me', or maybe, don't cling, hands off
love, or even, no, don't grab at my feet.

For when we turn to Gospel stories about Jesus of Nazareth's
relationships with women, we hear of some such uninhibited and
determined and even passionate meetings. To stay only with the
stories which came to be associated with Mary of Magdala, it's
one thing to imagine a culture in which a guest might be cared for
by providing him with scented oils to clean dust from face and
hair, or to soothe sore feet, but a woman *weeping* over his feet in
public, and drying them with her long, braided hair, surely marks
her out as given to absurdly extravagent gesture. She's capable of
causing acute embarrassment – unless of course, the tables are
turned on her critics. Thus in Luke's Gospel:

> I entered your house, you gave me no water for my feet, but she
> has wet my feet with her tears, and wiped them with her hair.
> You gave me no kiss, but from the time I came in she has not
> ceased to kiss my feet. You did not anoint my head with oil, but
> she has anointed my feet with ointment.

It's as though someone were saying, John Baptist didn't think he
was worthy to unlatch Jesus' shoes, but *she* was, and why?
Because what Jesus recognized in her was that she had thrown
herself on the mercy and love of God. This point above all, was
central to the association of this text from Luke with Mary of
Magdala, who became the symbol of penitence, a penitence
flowing from complete assurance of mercy and love, and *not*,
ever, from condemnation. So her apparent extravagence is
matched by his generosity, his unstinting praise.

And next, if you recall that in the garden, outside the tomb,
Mary responds to her name with one word, 'Rabboni', Teacher,
we can connect that with the story of another Mary, sitting at his
feet, learning from him the way a disciple might learn from a
rabbi – not completely unheard of for a woman, but very unusual.
So we begin, I think, to get some clues as to why women disciples
would travel with him, some of them acting as a kind of back-up
team, very necessary if he wasn't to walk around half-starved,

scavenging raw grain from the edges of fields. It's no surprise then, to find them as close as they dared stay throughout the brutality of the crucifixion, and doing what they could to care for the wreck of his body – here are the tears and the cleansing oils again, but for the last possible time, for a man well beyond returning delighted praise for uninhibited appreciation. For those who watched and waited, Mary of Magdala among them, the final letting go of what was left of Jesus was going to hurt very badly. Blind with tears, Mary turns away from the tomb, sees someone standing, trusts him to tell her what she wants to know, recognizes him when he responds to her need of him by saying her name. She finds not death but life, in an astonishing reversal of her expectation, finds herself in the presence of the Christ she loves, and who loves her, and is freed from hanging on to him, able to bear this leavetaking.

Or at least, that's how this exchange between them seems to have been read in the tradition. For commentators reached for words from the Song of Songs to attribute to her in their meditation on this Gospel material.

> I will rise now and go about the city,
> in the streets and in the squares;
> I will seek him whom my soul loves.
> I sought him, but found him not.
> Oh, that you were like a brother to me,
> that nursed at my mother's breast!
> If I met you outside, I would kiss you,
> and none would despise me.
> I would lead you and bring you
> into the house of my mother.
> Rejoice with me, all you who love the Lord,
> for I sought him and he appeared to me.
> And while I was weeping at the tomb, I saw my
> Lord. Alleluia.

Mary thus becomes a new Eve, loved, blessed and graced with life-giving words, 'I have seen the Lord', and so named apostle to the apostles in the church's tradition.

I've deliberately drawn on stories across the Gospels, homilies on the Gospels, and all sorts of traditions and interpretations to weave around this story. Even if we scrape them all away, and restrict ourselves only to Mary of Magdala's presence near the crucified one, her presence at the tomb, and this extraordinary exchange with the risen Christ, one central point remains. Like it or not, in the communities for which this Gospel was written, the apostolic authority of being first witness to the resurrection faith of the Christian tradition, whatever we in our turn make of it, is associated with this woman. In chapter 4 of John, in the very different story of Jesus' encounter with the Samaritan woman, there's a curiously incomplete moment when the disciples, surprised and baffled by the freedom and openness of his dealings with her did not dare to ask him, 'What do you want of a woman?' – a question capable of receiving many different answers. But this text in John 20 gives us one answer, and we could I think say that it is a question whose time has come in the institutional church where this Gospel is still read.

Yet resurrection is a sense of direction,
resurrection is a bee-line,

straight to the horde and plunder,
the treasure, the store-room,

the honeycomb,
resurrection is resurrection,

food, shelter, fragrance
of myrrh and balm.[1]

[1] HD, 'The Flowering of the Rod', *Trilogy*, Carcanet Press 1973.

Ann Loades

GOD'S GOOD GREENING POWER

Hildegard of Bingen's gift of Veriditas

The Word
is living,
being,
spirit,
all verdant greening,
all creativity.
All creation
is awakened,
called,
by the resounding melody,
God's invocation of the Word.
This Word manifests in every creature.[1]

These words were written in the twelfth century by an extraordinarily gifted theologian, mystic and artist whom most Christians have never heard of. For eight hundreds years, Hildegard of Bingen has been virtually unknown in the West, even though her achievement is comparable to that of such familiar mediaeval saints as Thomas Aquinas or St Anselm. Significantly, it took a secular female artist, Judy Chicago, to rediscover Hildegard in the early 1980s,[2] and only now, very belatedly, is the church waking up to one of its most gifted children.

Born in 1098 in the valley of the Nahe in the Rhineland, Hildegard was tithed to God and sent at the age of eight to live with Jutta, a holy anchoress attached to the abbey of St Disibode. At about the age of eighteen she took the Benedictine habit and then, later in 1136 when Jutta died, she became abbess of the community. All through her early life, Hildegard was plagued by terrible sickness and was confined to bed for long periods – no doubt as a result of the repression of her extraordinary gifts, since, for more than forty years, she tells us, 'she refused to write' out of a false humility and 'because of doubt and erroneous thinking', not to mention 'controversial advice from men'! Finally, divinity itself seems to have grown impatient with Hildegard's condition of passive muteness and determined to break into her silence. In her forty-second year, she had the first of what became a whole series of remarkable visions, in which she saw a great brilliance out of which a voice from heaven commanded her: 'O weak person, you who are both ashes of ashes and decaying of decaying, speak and write what you see and hear ...' In obedience, Hildegard put her hand to writing and immediately, she tells us, 'a deep and profound exposition of books came over me.'[3] For the rest of her life, till she died at the age of eighty-one, Hildegard's creativity flowed in a ceaseless spate of books – on theology, medicine, science, physiology and poetry – as well as in her visions and illuminations, in preaching, teaching, administration and composing. She was renowned throughout Europe for her learning and wisdom, and was not averse to ticking off the Pope or the Emperor for their failings.

One of Hildegard's most vivid concepts, and one which is most pertinent to our time, is her notion of 'Veriditas', a word she made up, meaning 'greening power', which runs like a stream through all her writing. Centuries before 'green' politics and spirituality became trendy, Hildegard championed an entire theology of greening power which might arguably have changed the course of Western Christianity and culture, had her wisdom been heeded rather than relegated to obscurity. It may not be too strong to suggest that we are now paying the price for ignoring Hildegard – and others who shared her compassion for creation.

Greenness in Hildegard's thought is 'God's freshness that humans receive in their spiritual and physical life-forces. It is the power of springtime, a germinating force, a fruitfulness that comes from God and permeates all creation'. She talks of 'the exquisite greening of trees and grasses', of 'earth's lush greening'. She says that all of creation and humanity in particular is 'showered with greening refreshment, the vitality to bear fruit'. She believes that Christ brings 'lush greenness' to 'shrivelled and wilted' people and institutions. She celebrates the Divine Word as 'all verdant greening, all creativity'. She calls God 'the purest spring', and the Holy Spirit is greening power in motion, making all things grow, expand, celebrate. Indeed, for Hildegard salvation or healing is the return of greening power and moistness. She celebrates this in her opera, *Ordo Virtutum*. 'In the beginning all creatures were green and vital; they flourished amidst flowers. Later the green figure itself came down.' Thus Jesus himself is called 'Greenness Incarnate'.[4]

Hildegard's understanding of Veriditas is rooted in a love and celebration of the created order which Christians in our time desperately need to cultivate. There is no dualism here, no fateful splitting apart of spirit and flesh which has so plagued Western Christianity and culture. Rather, the earth is affirmed as God's handiwork, mother of all life, and, most wonderful of all, very stuff of which the Son took flesh in the incarnation:

> The earth is ... mother,
> she is mother of all that is natural,
> mother of all that is human.
> She is the mother of all,
> for contained in her
> are the seeds of all.
> The earth of humankind
> contains all moisture,
>   all verdancy,
>   all germinating power.
> It is in so many ways
> fruitful.
> All creation comes from it.
> Yet it forms not only the basic
> raw material of humankind,
> but also the substance of
> the incarnation
> of God's son.[5]

Hildegard's understanding of the lush greening power of God in creation can transform our theology and spirituality in many ways. For now, perhaps I might suggest three implications of Hildegard's notion of greenness for our faith.

First, Hildegard helps us see that our faith and our prayer is, or should be, *earthy*. If God's Word is in all creation, if the Word is the one who adorns all the earth, if the earth is mother of all and substance of the incarnation itself, then far from fleeing from the earth in order to pray and find God, we need rather to fling ourselves joyfully into it, to open our eyes and ears to God's presence in creation, to cherish and celebrate all God's creatures as living words which may speak God's wisdom to us. Thus Eckhart declares 'Every creature is a word of God and is a book about God'. Or, as Gerard Manley Hopkins put it, 'The world is charged with the grandeur of God'.

Second, Hildegard helps us see that our faith and our prayer should be *passionate, sensual, bodily*. If matter is declared good and lovely by God, is loved so much that the Son takes flesh in order to reveal God to us, then we can know that *our* bodies and flesh are good and lovely too. Prayer is not to be perceived as flight from the body, subjugation of the flesh, denial of the passions, as it so often has been in the past, so much as a celebration of the senses, the integration and right ordering of our desires, learning to cultivate the wisdom of the body. 'Do not disdain your body' says Mechtild of Magdeburg, 'for the soul is just as safe in the body as in the kingdom of heaven'. Or, as Francis of Assisi might put it, with his lovely metaphor for the body, don't kick and abuse Brother Ass: feed, water and cherish him, and he will carry you. Spirit and body are not opposites in tension with each other, but work together to serve and praise God.

Finally, Hildegard helps us to see that our faith can and should be *open to knowledge and wisdom about our world*, wherever it comes from; especially she helps us to see how Christian faith needs to prize and revere the gifts and insights of scientists, artists and mystics, whatever tradition they come from. Too often in the past the church has been fearful and condemning of the advances of knowledge, and has paid a heavy price for its carping suspicion. Hildegard's life and work is a glorious testimony to the oneness of all wisdom. She believed passionately that all truth belongs to God and leads to God. As Matthew Fox puts it, she 'brings together the holy trinity of art, science and religion'. Fox goes on: 'Einstein warned that "science without religion is lame; religion without science is blind". Hildegard would surely concur. But she would add that science and religion without art are ineffective and violent; and art without science and religion is vapid.'[6] In our time, when the explosion of knowledge has led to a splitting apart of the disciplines, we need even more desperately than Hildegard's time did a vision of the unity of knowledge if we are to respond to the needs of the planet and nurture life on earth in the fullness for which God intends it.

In a letter written to her sisters late in her life, Hildegard talks about her death and she expresses her wish that 'my voice may never fall into forgetfulness among you; may it rather be heard often in your midst in love'.[7] It is a terrible tragedy and injustice that Hildegard's voice, along with so many other wise and gifted voices of women, has been forgotten for all these centuries of Western history. But perhaps it is not too late. Perhaps at long last the church and the world are ready to hear what Hildegard has to teach us. Let us pray that it may be so.

1   Gabriele Uhlein (ed.), *Meditations with Hildegard of Bingen*, Bear & Co.1983, p. 49.
2   See Judy Chicago, *The Dinner Party: A Symbol of our Heritage*, Double-day 1979, pp. 75ff.
3   Quoted in Matthew Fox (ed.), *Illuminations of Hildegard of Bingen*, Bear & Co.1985, p. 27.
4   *Illuminations*, pp. 31–32.
5   *Meditations*, p. 58.
6   *Illuminations*, p. 14, 15.
7   *Illuminations*, p. 13.

Nicola Slee

A SERMON FOR ST JOHN'S, HAMPSTEAD*

Jeremiah 33.6–9; John 17.11–23; Ephesians 4.1–6

I must apologize. I'm late. Actually I'm four hundred years late. It's taken me that long to find my way from what is represented by the IBVM community house at 47 Fitzjohn's Avenue to your church and all it represents. Mary Ward, the Englishwoman who founded our community here in London in 1606 when she first gathered a group of like-minded friends around her, was born in 1585. The church and nation in which she was reared pitted

---

* Preached during the Week of Prayer for Christian Unity.

Christians against each other. As a Roman Catholic she had to flee to the continent to get her nascent religious community off the ground. Meanwhile Robert Browne, the truculent dissenter, was busy writing *A Treatise of Reformation without Tarrying for Anie* and – chillingly – *A Booke which Showeth the Life and Manners of all True Christians*. Blessedly, the *via media* opened up between the two as the true anglican way. When I tell you that Mary Ward's first sisters were persecuted from within the Catholic Church as 'galloping gurles' who 'gad about in town and country' and because they laboured 'like priests'; when I tell you that Mary Ward wrote prophetically in 1616 that 'women in time to come will do much'; when I tell you that her deepest desire was the conversion of England – you may decide you don't like her very much after all. And that you don't think that I was late enough. Another four hundred years would have done quite nicely.

But that's when I have to remind you that you've already met her. You know her in Sisters Stephen and Callista who wander all over Hampstead, and particularly to the Royal Free, and always have the right word for everyone. You know her in Sister Gertrude who brings her generous and loving heart to your prayer meetings. You know her in Sisters Philippa and Catherine from their work at Eden Hall. You know her in Sisters Richard, Madeleine and Jude because some of your children have been taught by them. You know her in the rest of us because we have been living in your parish for over fifty years. You have seen us around and somehow, indirectly, you must have known that we were praying for you and your homes and all who live with you. Even if, seditiously, we are inspired by someone who had an exalted theology of what it is to be a woman in the church, by someone who desired the conversion of England.

I have said I am four hundred years late; as a woman who writes about Christian spirituality, I am also eighty years late. There is a grave in your cemetery of which you have reason to feel especially proud. It contains the remains of Mrs Moore. Of course Archibishop Ramsey couldn't say enough about her. After all she was the most the prolific religious writer of this century, the first woman to lecture at Oxford, a fellow of King's College here in London, the first Anglican laywoman to give retreats, a religious editor of the *Spectator*. What Ramsey in fact claimed was that she did more than anyone else in Anglicanism to keep the spiritual life alive between the wars. That means that she taught clergymen like your vicar to say their prayers better – or perhaps I mean to say their prayers. She is buried with her husband. Their gravestone reads: H. Stuart Moore and his wife Evelyn, daughter of Sir Arthur Underhill.

To give a flavour of Evelyn Underhill's writings, I quote:

Perhaps some of you have read Dr Doolittle's Circus, a book which is nearly as full of spiritual wisdom as Alice in Wonderland. There is, you remember, one admirable member of the circus; a most steady and responsible creature called Sophy the Wise Seal. But unfortunately Sophy had a husband, whose name was Slushy. Now in the spiritual life Sophy is one of the best and most reliable of companions; but we have to keep a very sharp look-out for Slushy. He has his pious moments, when he tries to push his quiet wife on one side and suggest to us what a helpful animal he is – such a good appearance, so fervent, and so full of feeling. But Slushy, like all sentimentalists, is really a very self-indulgent creature. What he calls zest is mostly feverishness; and what he calls worship is mostly basking. There are some devotional books in which one seems to hear nothing but Slushy flapping his tail; just as in others the quiet wise Sophy finds a few humble words, which yet convey her utter submission to God. Slushy, though at first sight very attractive, with his warm devotional colour and soft fur, is really wrapped up in nothing better than his own feelings. Sophy may not have such a good coat; but she keeps in much better condition, because she looks at herself and her own feelings very little, and at God and the mighty purposes of God and the needs of the children of God a very great deal. It is by keeping company with Sophy, sharing her point of view and sense of proportion, that we shall achieve a deep, healthy, self-forgetful inner life.[1]

As your church legislates this year about the proper role of women, the proper place of women amongst the ranks of the ordained, please remember the heroic labours of Mary Ward's first sisters. As the words 'cost of conscience' and feelings become, as it were, interchangeable, please remember the cool lucid voice of Evelyn Underhill.

But let us remember too the appeal of today's readings. As we begin the week of prayer for Christian Unity, Jeremiah reminds us that healing lies in God's gift. The author of the Letter to the Ephesians calls us to the unity of the Spirit in the bond of peace and in John's Gospel we learn of the desire of Jesus for oneness.

The Blessed Trinity models unity for us. In our quest for Christian unity, our pilgrimages – now on a road to Compostella, now on a road to Jerusalem, now fearing a road to Rome – we forget that Christ is the road we travel: the way and truth and life who will lead us to our journey's end. Neither Mary Ward with her dream of the conversion of England nor the Non-Conformist Robert Browne with his dream of reformation need register alarm. The life of the Trinity offers no compromise; it demands all and offers all. Unity is about mutuality, acceptance and love.

I close with Helen Waddell's astonishing translation of Boethius' prayer to the Trinity – a prayer we could very well make our own in Christian Unity week:

O Father, give the spirit power to climb
To the fountain of all light, and be purified.
Break through the mists of earth, the weight of the clod,
Shine forth in splendour, Thou that art calm weather,
And quiet resting place for faithful souls.
To see Thee is the end and the beginning.
Thou carriest us, and Thou dost go before
Thou art the journey, and the journey's end.[2]

[1] From Evelyn Underhill, *Collected Papers*, quoted in Lavinia Byrne (ed.), *The Hidden Tradition*, SPCK 1991, p. 111.

[2] From Dame Felicitas Corrigan, *Helen Waddell*, quoted in *The Hidden Tradition*, pp. 93–4.

Lavinia Byrne IBVM

IN SOLIDARITY WITH WOMEN*

There was a marvellous time in the history of the people of Israel, a special and a precious time

> when they first entered into the promised land;
> when they first realized that God's promises had come true;
> and before they wanted to be like the other nations;
> before they wanted a king;
> before they wanted the security of knowing which human being – which man (for kings can only be men) would be ruling over them next.

And in those precious early days, the Lord's spirit would fall upon a chosen leader of Israel, someone chosen to lead the people through a time of crisis. One of those chosen of God was the leader whose song we shared earlier in this service. It was Deborah,

> the judge over Israel,
> the one who brought God's word to the people of Israel,
> who led them to a great and a glorious victory
> – *her* people, she led to victory.

There was another precious and golden time, when the Christ had come, and the final victory had been won. We have seen in dance, and we have heard in scripture and song how Jesus was laid in the tomb, how the stone was rolled across the entrance to the tomb and he was dead ...

> and then they came, and the tomb was empty and the final victory
>> over death
>> over sin
> the final barrier had been rolled way,
> the final victory had been won.

And who was it that Jesus sent to take as apostles that first message?

* A sermon given at the outset of the WCC Decade for the Churches, at Westminster Abbey on the Sunday after Easter 1988.

It was Mary, and Salome, and Joanna. They went at Jesus' behest, and they told the others, and gradually the message spread, until that glorious day when the spirit of God fell upon God's people, and the sons and the daughters of God's people began to prophesy – to proclaim God's message.

After each of those very precious times, there came a deadening. There came an institutionalization.

> After all, God, we're only human: we like security; we like rules and regulations; we like to know exactly where we are; we like to be like the nations.

– and the people of Israel wanted to know who was going to be their ruler next ...

> It's all very well trusting God, but you never know who he's going to choose. It's all very well letting go of the security and taking the adventure that God gives, but it takes a lot of courage, and we are only human.

So we've done rather well really, haven't we? I mean we've made a wonderful institution out of God's great truths. We have hedged God's wonderful message around with *all sorts* of lovely logical rules and regulations, so that God knows who to choose and who not to choose, (after all, he might get it wrong on his own).

We've even taken the glorious message that thunders from the pages of scripture and we have reinterpreted it. We have maimed and tortured and twisted – look at the Greek of Paul's letters, and what translators have done to it – and with the wreckage we have reassembled the barriers that Christ died to destroy. HOW DARE WE?

How dare any human being stand before God and say:

> *him* you may choose, but *her*, God, you *may not* choose?

Will you tell God on whom God may pour the spiritual gifts? Will you take issue with God?

I am an ordained minister – have been for nearly nine years now (as in 1988) – and I come from a tradition, the congregational, or independent tradition, which has ordained women as well as men since 1917 in this country: earlier in the States. I stand in a line of women and men who have been called of God and have taken up that ordained ministry. What if those *women* had kept, or had been kept silent? What are we doing when we silence the voice of people whom God is calling?

And it's worse than that, because the church – God's people as a whole – has a calling to fulfil. This is not only – or even primarily about ordained ministry.

We are called to demonstrate in our lives, individually and in community,
we are called to demonstrate the new creation,
God's eternal reign in and through God's people.
We are called to be witnesses to that new creation
to fulfil once again the purpose of God's creation of human beings

male and female we were created in the image of God.

What do we do? *We split the image.*
Here is the fullness of life. Here is the vision that is before us:

the vision of a community

a resurrection community living with the life that Christ gives –
in which individuals can stand strong and free in the graces and
the gifts which God has given

women and men working and witnessing and worshipping together.

This is the vision.
We may fail. We very often do. *But we needn't build failure into the rules by which we run the thing.*
In this decade for the church in solidarity with women, it is not our aim to be sectarian. We are hoping to reopen the doors – no, we are hoping to reopen the *floodgates*

so that the spirit and the power of God may pour into this world through a redeemed community of God's people

so that God may raise up women and men
to work for God in this world

to live and demonstrate the great and wonderful message of redemption and resurrection, and liberation.

Have we got the courage to accept that vision? Have we got the courage to allow God to choose? If so, then we can go forward in God's spirit, in God's might, in God's love, to the glory of the name of our God. Amen.

Janet Wootton

BY THE WATERS OF BABYLON*

By the waters of Babylon we sat down and wept when we
    remembered Zion
As for our harps we hung them up on the trees that are in the
    land.
For there those who led us away captive required of us a song:
    and those who had despoiled us demanded mirth saying
    sing us one of the songs of Zion.

How can we sing the Lord's song in a strange land? (Ps. 137.1–4)

When people are oppressed they tend to get depressed. And the longer and the more heavily they are oppressed the more depressed they are likely to become. The depression becomes a very effective way of keeping the oppression in place with no effort on the part of the oppressor. The depression of the oppressed keeps their oppression in place.

Any of you who have any experience of depression will know as I know how hard it is to do anything much when you are depressed – it's certainly not a time when we think of taking on people we find difficult, people we are angry with, situations we want to change. Often all we want to do when we are depressed is just sit and be miserable. We feel trapped, unable to move, helpless, victims, totally dependant on others for help.

*A sermon given at St Matthew's, Brixton in August 1986.

The people of Israel as they sat by the waters of Babylon felt trapped, helpless, victims. And in many senses they were. The Hebrews, oppressed by Pharaoh in Egypt too felt like this – trapped, helpless, victims, and in many senses they were. Many black people in South Africa and here in this country have felt like this for many years, trapped, helpless, victims and in many senses they have been and are. I and many women in the Church of England have felt like this for some years and particularly in the last few weeks and in many senses we have been.

But if we remain in our depression the oppression does not disappear, the oppression grows instead, it grows stronger and our depression grows with it. Look at Egypt look at Babylon, look at South Africa, look at our country, look at our church. Our depression can hold us in place, keep us trapped, helpless, victims just as surely as our oppression. There may be times when we are victims, when we are trapped – for example when we are young, when people physically stronger than us hold us down by force, or when we are outnumbered. But we are not called as human beings to be helpless powerless, victims. We are not called to suffer over and over again needlessly.

Powerless victims go on being victims for ever, powerless victims end up dead and buried and achieve nothing. We are called to life, to abundant life, to life in all its fullness. If we *choose* to be weak, vulnerable powerless, this can only be in order to smash the cycle of oppression, to change things, to open up for ourselves and others full abundant life. This is what Jesus did – he was not a powerless victim, he made a powerful choice – in order to change things. He embraced and welcomed death to receive and bring life, not to wallow in suffering and in being a powerless victim.

Anything which continues our own or anyone else's oppression must be resisted not cultivated as so often in the church. Suffering should never be cultivated or sought after. The gospel is about Life, life for all, the gospel is about liberation, liberation for all. The gospel is about the end of oppression, the end of oppression for all.

A few weeks ago the General Synod of the Church of England decided to refuse to allow women priests lawfully ordained overseas to celebrate the eucharist in churches in England. Male priests from overseas of course continue to be welcome. At the same synod, though it was agreed women could become deacons, the ordination of women to the priesthood was postponed yet again despite the agreement of several years ago that there is no fundamental objection to the ordination of women to the priesthood.

I decided that I had sat down by the waters of Babylon and wept for long enough. Enough is enough. I am taking down my harp from the trees and I am playing it. I am singing the Lord's song even if it is in a strange land.

I love the Church of England. It has been part and parcel of my life since I was born. My father is, and my mother's father was, an Anglican priest. I was paid to work for the Church of England for fourteen years. I have taught, I have preached I have helped train future priests (male priests). I have over and over again worked to change the church from within; I have believed what I have been told over and over again that the only way to change something is from inside. But enough is enough.

Just as the Hebrews in Egypt decided enough was enough, I and many women are deciding enough is enough. We do not have to go on and on being victims, we do not have to go on allowing ourselves to be oppressed, we do not have to go on allowing ourselves to be depressed. We no longer need to hang up our harps.

Three years ago thirteen women left Southwark cathedral just after receiving communion at an ordination service – we left to celebrate a wilderness liturgy outside the cathedral. We were enacting a decision to go into the wilderness, to leave the oppression of Egypt behind, to refuse to continue to be victims. It was around that time that I stopped working for the Church of England. Since then although I have never since been to an ordination service, I have continued to worship, receive and administer communion and preach in Anglican churches. Though I have been in the wilderness I have received from and have kept connections with the oppressors. A month ago I decided that I had to sever yet another connection. I decided that I could no longer continue to receive communion from male priests in a church which continues to oppress women so badly, in a church which refuses to test my or any other woman's vocation to the priesthood in the way that it tests men's.

I began to question my own vocation (even more than I always do). Perhaps God is calling me more to a prophetic than a priestly ministry? Most of the prophets were on the edge, on the outside, over against the institution. Perhaps this is my vocation, at least for the moment.

Not receiving communion makes the wilderness more of a wilderness in some senses. I have found it very painful on three occasions, not receiving communion with my friends and fellow Anglicans, I shall find it particularly difficult this morning. But I want to claim life. I do not want to go on being a victim. I do not want to go on pretending, hiding and suppressing my feelings, my beliefs. It is hard to turn my back on an organization, on a community of people I love but it would be even harder to go on living a lie. I want to witness in my not receiving communion to the brokenness of our community, to make this visible rather than pretend that everything is all right.

I want to end by praying in the words of a collect written this week by a friend of mine, Janet Morley. I pray there words here with you my friends.

O covenant God,
You call us to the risk of commitment,
even from the place of despair,
As Ruth and Naomi loved and held on to one another,
abandoning the ways of the past,
So may we also not be divided,
but travel together into that strange land,
where you will lead us.
Amen.[1]

From a Wilderness Liturgy: Petertide 1983[2]

The Hebrews in Egypt groaned under the oppression of the Pharaohs. They were oppressed greatly and any attempts to resist oppression were met with even greater oppression. They cried out in their oppression and God heard their cry. He called them out of Egypt away from their oppression. The only way for the Hebrews to get out from under the weight of oppression was for them to leave it behind, to move away from it, to refuse to be oppressed any longer.

Perhaps there is a message for us here today.

The Hebrews left the oppression behind but they also left behind security, safety and comfort. At least they had known where they were in Egypt. It may not have been entirely pleasant but at least it was relatively secure and comfortable. They went out from Egypt into the wilderness where there was no security, no safety, no comfort. In the wilderness all they had was each other, God and the few things they had managed to bring with them from Egypt.

Perhaps there is a message for us here today.

The wilderness is stark, cruel, bare and lonely. There is nowhere to hide in the wilderness – either from each other or from God. The bare necessities of life suddenly become precious, love, food, drink, shelter. Life was tough for the Hebrews in the wilderness so tough they wished they were back in Egypt where at least they'd had the bare necessities of life.

Perhaps there is a message for us here today.

Yes the wilderness is tough, it is cruel, it is stark. In the wilderness we are brought up against the stark realities of life. In the wilderness we see God face to face, there is no escape. In the wilderness we depend on each other to a much greater extent. *But* the Hebrews were not neglected in the wilderness; it did feel terrible, lonely and uncomfortable but God did supply food, God did supply food, God did supply drink, God did supply comfort.

Perhaps there is a message for us here today.

The wilderness seemed and seems endless; life in the wilderness is tough and difficult, but the wilderness is *not* endless and there *are* oases in the wilderness. Out of the experience of the wilderness comes new life. The Hebrews wandered in the wilderness, were uncomfortable in the wilderness for a long time. But the people of Israel, the chosen race, grew from the experience of the wilderness.

Perhaps there is a message for us here today.

God *called* the people of Israel out of Egypt out of oppression and led them into the wilderness. God *called* Jesus at his baptism and drove him into the wilderness. Out of the wilderness emerged the first Israel, out of the wilderness emerged the new Israel of Jesus.

Some of us feel called by God, some of us feel driven out of the church and into the wilderness. We don't know what will emerge out of our wilderness, we feel our wilderness is endless, but *let's* wait on God in our wilderness – open and ready for the food God gives us in the wilderness.

[1]   A revised version of this prayer appears in *All Desires Known*, SPCK 1992.
[2]   The liturgy at which this sermon was preached originally appeared in *Celebrating Women*, Movement for the Ordination of Woman/Women in Theology 1986.

Bridget Rees

5

Speaking into the Silence

Themes associated with silence and speaking lie at the centre of this work and it is appropriate to state them in their most radical form in this concluding section.

We have already explored ways in which our bodily experiences and restricted access to economic and cultural power may generate particular insights in women and give us a 'different' voice in which to speak from the pulpit. We have noted that this can be a threatening gift to contribute when it disturbs a consensus based on ideas of a 'common' human experience or touches on difficult social issues which are usually repressed in Christian public speech. However, these challenges begin to appear minor when compared to the deep re-visioning that accompanies a critical approach by women to the 'common store' of myth and metaphor upon which our understanding of the world is based.

Anthropological studies have shown us how human beings make sense of their existence by referring to a treasured resource of sacred myths, folk lore and proverbial wisdom which functions as a mirror to daily life. Through it we can see and understand our own experiences, place them in broader perspective and add new insights to the library of human knowledge.

These stories are not written on stone but may be retold differently as need arises. We use the mythology of ancient Greece, for example, as a resource for understanding personality problems and mental illness – the tale of Oedipus lives on in the Oedipus complex. This process, however, is fraught with difficulty for women because the 'common store' from which we draw resources to interpret our living has been collected and canonized by men. Whether it is the epic of the Trojan wars, the stories of the Hebrew scriptures or the wit and wisdom of our own day, women inhabit a shadowy realm in mythology as the disruptive bringers of chaos, the unmoved movers of great events, the passive victims of circumstances. We are unable to see reflected our experience of being creators, actors and subjects in our own right rather than the secondary counterparts of men. Writing on this subject in her book *Diving Deep and Surfacing*, Carol Christ states:

> In a very real sense there is no experience without stories. Stories give shape to experience, experience gives rise to stories … At least this is how it is for those who have had the freedom to tell their own stories, to shape them in accord with their experience. This has not usually been the case for women. Indeed there is a very real sense in which the seemingly paradoxical statement 'women have not experienced their own experience' is true.

The question of women's relation to myths and metaphors is of course related to that of our approach to the texts of scripture, and we will see women preachers using similar strategies in relation to both. There are nevertheless important differences. In regard to biblical texts it is possible, for example, for critics like Phyllis Trible to argue in a convincing scholarly way that we have misinterpreted the story of Adam and Eve. She suggests that the Christian community should amend its understanding of this ancient tale and re-tell it in ways less injurious to women. However, her academic arguments do not reach out to subvert the popular understandings of the story that have grown up around the biblical text over centuries. This is where the 'story' lives and also where its destructive power is most keenly felt.

Yet, ironically, precisely because myths live through repeated common use rather than because they are fixed on a printed page they prove a more flexible medium in which to work than scripture. Furthermore, when women of faith begin to turn their attention to myths and archetypes they find themselves in the company of other women who might not give their attention to specifically theological concerns but who operate on a wider cultural stage. We have much to gain by gathering insights from women's literature and literary theory as we trace the way women preachers may become the active creators of a new mythology.

Alicia Ostriker, an American poet and critic, has made a study of the ways in which many women writers have acted as thieves of language, raiding the resources of myths and fables and using the powerful symbols they contain to create stories which more accurately mirror their experience. She pictures scriptural and legendry epics as 'fence-posts' marking out a sacred realm of spiritual truth without being identical to it. As such the human heritage of sacred mythology cannot simply be ignored because we recognize that it marks out holy ground but neither will women feel compelled to treat the myths themselves as sacred or inviolable.

With women poets we look at or into but not up at sacred things, we unlearn submission.

She claims that throughout history women have attempted to subvert the myths upon which society rests, but to protect themselves from censure they have denied the radical implications of this process by claiming to be interpreters rather than re-shapers of tradition. We have disguised 'passion as piety, rebellion as obedience'.

In our own days women are beginning to have the self confidence and the power to be open about their re-telling of ancient myths and their creation of new ones. The poet HD powerfully reshapes the characters of Helen of Troy and Mary of Magdala and gives them a central position in her epic poetry. The French feminist author, Helene Cixous, framed a polemical call to women to begin to tell their own stories. She entitled her essay 'The Laugh of the Medusa' thus indicating her belief that the time has come when we must cease to fear women's power and creativity and look boldly into each other's faces – 'the Medusa is beautiful and she is laughing'. On a more popular level Alice Walker's novel *The Color Purple* has become an important alternative 'Odyssey' for many women; recounting a black woman's pilgrimage in the struggle against racism and abuse to the point where she is able to stand upright, to love other women and to name God for herself.

By and large these developments in feminist literature have remained unnoticed by the theological mainstream but increasingly feminist theologians are coming to see themselves as engaged in a common project with visionary women writers. They, in turn, see their work as a spiritual task and may refer to themselves as mystics, mediums and prophetic messengers – claiming an ancient heritage.

It may be that through these endeavours new life can be generated from old (and apparently barren) religious forms but it would be foolish to underestimate the disruption that would accompany this creative renewal. Instead of 'orthodox' statements of the faith a rich and creative 'muddle' would emerge as the Christian story began to be told in many voices. Furthermore, it would be clear that women were not merely reviving used traditions but creating new 'holy pictures' through a process of 'theo-phantasy' – imagining the sacred.

Such an open process of artistic creation is unauthorized within our tradition and is bound to appear as a scandal to many. Nevertheless, despite the strictures that surround the way faith material may be handled, many women preachers are beginning to create new stories as vehicles for communicating their experience and their faith.

Because it is difficult to obtain a platform (or pulpit) from which to speak as a woman in the church, many of us exercise self restraint and caution in 'myth-making' in order to remain within the fold. Others more keen that new stories be told whatever the cost may seek platforms to communicate the stories we are creating outside the church. Quite often women move between worlds presenting new stories in traditional ways from the pulpit on Sundays and sharing more threatening material at conferences, special services and in close feminist groups. Material from these different contexts has been included in this section of the book and the contributions also show the wide range of strategies women may employ in their construction of new traditions.

Margaret Hebblethwaite's sermon reminds us that space has long existed within mainstream Christianity to 'imagine' the gospel and to place our own experience in the Christian story. Her call is to value and use this potential for our own enrichment. Mary Cotes 'retells' the story of David and the Prophet Nathan in a way that reminds us we are usually blind to the female figure of Bathsheba around whose abduction and sexual use the story turns. When she is included in the story the terms of the easy resolution between Prophet and King are questioned.

The strategy behind Heather Walton's narrative sermon is to expose the powerful presuppositions at work in the way the story of the annunciation is usually told and to disturb a tale of placid receptive obedience by confronting it with one in which a woman articulates her passion and terror. Janet Lees moves beyond the framework provided by the original text when creating her 'midrash' of the three wise women. She does not apologize for her theo-phantasy but confidently constructs it in such a way as to bring new meaning to an over familiar legend. Similarly, Hazel Walton uses a powerful biblical metaphor as a basis for a striking new narrative.

The final two contributions from Sarah Maitland and Alison Webster also build confidently upon the creative imagination, but in different ways. 'Bad Friday' requires us to respond with our own imaginative power to the invitation of the story-teller and assumes this process to be an entirely appropriate act of Christian devotion. In contrast Alison Webster sets a work of female imagination, *Oranges are not the Only Fruit* by Jeanette Winterson, against the established male tradition and claims greater authority for the former than the latter. Her work carries a reminder that this practice may close the doors of the churches to women who dare to take the process of 'experiencing their own experience' this far.

All the sermons speak into our silence and offer examples for the woman preacher to follow as far as she may dare.

SERMON TO ST ANDREWS*

John 1.29–40

It is customary for the Sunday after Epiphany to celebrate the baptism of Jesus. And that is the tradition I am following, though the Gospel account of the baptism given in John's version is a

---

* A sermon given to St Andrews University at the beginning of term, January 1990.

memory recounted by the Baptist rather than the scene as it happens. The baptism of Jesus is a very suitable theme for the New Year: it is a theme of beginning – the beginning of Jesus' ministry. We also stand, of course, at the beginning of term, which gives a chance to make another new start, perhaps working harder than last term, or perhaps on the contrary playing harder.

One of my aims in this sermon is to open your minds to different ways of reading the Bible. We tend to be critical of fundamentalists for reading the Bible only one way and insisting that the literal way is the only way, and yet at times it seems that academic theologians can be just as restricted, as though their approach of textual analysis and criticism was the only valid way to read the Bible. Academic exegesis is fascinating and rich, and it can be exciting, but it is not the only way, nor even the only good way. I am going to speak about two other ways into the Gospel as well as the exegetical: I will call them the feminist, and the imaginative. There are other ways as well of reading the Gospel, but that will be plenty for one sermon.

Before going on to the feminist and imaginative approaches, let us begin by recalling how rich a background can be given by academic exegesis, for I do not in any way wish to undervalue the usefulness of this approach. In the passage from John's Gospel we learn a lot through looking at the concept of the 'lamb': John the Baptist points at Jesus and says 'Behold the Lamb of God'. This is the text that lies behind the many paintings that portray the Baptist – sometimes even shown as a child – pointing to a lamb. What is meant by 'lamb'? There are a number of associations, and I will draw your attention to three.

First we can draw attention to the Paschal lamb, the lamb of the Passover, which is sacrificed and eaten in the passover meal, and the blood of which saves the people from death when spread on the door posts (Ex. 12). So too Jesus is presented as one who will enable the people to pass from death to life, from slavery to freedom, from the old life to the new life. As St Paul says: 'Cleanse out the old leaven that you may be a new lump, as you really are unleavened. For Christ, our paschal lamb, has been sacrificed' (I Cor. 5.7). Secondly, we can refer to the suffering servant passage from Isaiah, in which we hear of someone who, though innocent, will suffer terribly on behalf of the people in order to bear their sins: 'He was oppressed and he was afflicted, yet he opened not his mouth; like a lamb that is led to the slaughter, and like a sheep that before its shearers is dumb, so he opened not his mouth' (Isa. 53.7). This is the very text picked up by Luke in Acts 8.32, when Philip explains to the Ethiopian eunuch how this text applies to Jesus. And thirdly, we can look forward in the scriptures to the Lamb of God in the book of Revelation – another work by the fourth evangelist or from his circle. The elders in heaven sing a new song to the Lamb: 'Worthy art thou to take the scroll and to open its seals, for thou wast slain and by thy blood didst ransom people for God ... Worthy is the Lamb who was slain, to receive power and wealth and wisdom and might and honour and glory and blessing' (Rev. 5.9,12). The great multitude in white robes have washed their robes white in the blood of the Lamb, which is a most vivid image of the same theological point, that is, that the sacrifice of the innocent Christ redeems and purifies us (7.14).

And so some exegesis of biblical themes and backgrounds can add richly to our understanding of the text, and these are only a few examples of what a little knowledge can bring.

I said I would also approach the text from a feminist perspective, and for this I would like to concentrate on another theme – the dove. 'I saw the Spirit descend as a dove from heaven,' says the Baptist, 'and it remained on him.' Like the Lamb it is a vivid image – both are white, soft, warm, living, and innocent.

Some of you may already know that the early Eastern fathers often spoke of the Holy Spirit as feminine, but you may not know that the reason for this, or at least the excuse for it, was the image of the dove. In Greek the word for dove is feminine – *peristera* – and so by speaking of the Spirit as 'the dove' the fathers are able to develop feminine language about God. Of course, writing in Greek every adjective will be in the feminine, agreeing with the noun, and at time the Fathers make full play of this, going on to use the idea of the dove as a mother. Here is such a passage from Gregory of Nyssa, a fourth-century eastern father, in which he speaks of our own baptism, building on the image of the dove descending and remaining on Jesus at his baptism:

Give the dove the opportunity to fly down upon you, she

whom Jesus, as our forerunner, first drew down from heaven: she who is without deceit, she who is gentleness, she who gives birth to many children. Whenever she finds someone cleansed, like a well-tended stove, she goes to live in him, and brooding over him she inflames his soul, and many and blessed are the children she bears. These are good deeds and holy words, faith, devotion, justice, self-control, chastity, purity (*Adv. eos qui differunt baptismum*, PG 46, 421B)

At the back of Gregory's mind, also, no doubt, is the beginning of Genesis, where the Spirit of God hovers over the face of the waters, using a word that is used of birds hovering over their nests. And the idea of brooding also draws on the repeated reference in John that the Spirit did not just descend on Jesus, but descended and remained: 'He on whom you see the Spirit descend and remain, this is he who baptizes with the Holy Spirit.' Where birds remain they brood, they warm into life, they are mothers.

But in any case the dove is easily seen as a female image, for its gentleness and grace. My son has a children's story about children sheltering in the warm feathers of a dove for safety: 'This wing seems like cream and a bit like a mother, when she lets us go to sleep in her arms at dusk ... We can entrust ourselves to the friendly dove, to the ancient dove who knows children and stays by them.'

Another modern female image of the dove comes to my mind: when I was in Nicaragua I was given a hand-cut wooden pendant as a symbol of the work done by the Committee of Mothers of Heroes and Martyrs – I have here a larger copy in felt. It shows a woman releasing a dove, and to me it seems a way of saying, 'women are the peace-makers', and at the same time, 'the Holy Spirit is the bearer of female qualities'. And I have a postcard from Brazil that uses a similar theme: titled 'Woman and Man: images of God' it shows a man on his knees looking up to heaven, while a woman standing at his side releases a couple of doves into the air. And I may add that when I was in Brazil at the Seventh Inter-ecclesial Meeting the standard form of address for God in prayer was 'God, our father and mother'. (I am aware of course, as I say this, that Scotland was the scene of some angry controversy in 1984 over the motherhood of God issue.)

Now we have looked at our gospel from a feminist perspective, albeit through the eyes of an ancient and revered father of the church, we can notice some differences in the kind of questions we are putting to scripture. In the exegetical approach we were asking, 'what was in the mind of the evangelist, that we might not notice without some background knowledge?' But when we explore the idea of the Spirit as mother-bird, we could imagine a Western European or North American exegete saying dismissively, 'but that was not in the mind of the evangelist'. To which we, and Gregory of Nyssa, can reply 'so what?' To accuse the fathers of unscholarly exegesis is to fail to understand what they were doing. Scripture is there to be ours, to work with and play with and pray with and enjoy and explore. It is the living word of God, to communicate with us now. It is written to change people's lives, not to be a dead text. Just as a play of Shakespeare is more truly itself when acted in the theatre rather than read in a book, so scripture is more truly itself when put into practice, when taken beyond itself and read in relationship with outside questions.

I said I would look also at another way into scripture, that I called the imaginative approach. What I have in mind here is what goes on in us when we pray on a passage of scripture rather than study it. It is a commonplace among spiritual directors that academics are often very bad at praying: when asked to reflect on what a text says to them they sometimes have a tendency to run away into abstract and learned reflections that do not touch them personally at all. They may have become so used to approaching scripture academically that they find it hard to relate to the Bible in any other way.

St Ignatius of Loyola, the sixteenth-century founder of the Jesuits, would encourage people in prayer to see themselves in a scene of scripture. This method of praying is known usually as Ignatian contemplation and has sometimes been described as the moment 'when you can feel the sand between your toes'. So then, if we pray on this scene with John the Baptist, we put ourselves there by the Jordan and see the scene, listen, smell, feel, and ask ourselves 'where do I find myself to be in this scene?' There was once a priest who admitted honestly to his spiritual director that in this particular scene he found himself to be John the Baptist and as each person came forward he pointed firmly toward Jesus: 'Behold the Lamb of God, go over there, that way,' he said to each, but meanwhile he noticed that he himself made no move at all in the direction of Jesus. He told others which way to go, but he did not go that way himself.

You can see from this example how this method of prayer can open us up to relate to God in a new way. The priest noticed something about himself he had not seen before. And having noticed it in this prayerful encounter with Christ through the scripture, the way was open for him to change, to let himself begin to move, to follow Jesus himself, to notice what it did to him inside when he became one of those who moved and followed, instead of one who stood still and felt good about telling others to move. You can see how learned thoughts about suffering servant imagery or echoes in the book of Revelation could become simply an alibi for such a person to avoid encountering the text in such a direct and life-transforming way. And after all the Gospels were written to change lives.

I have found from my experience of teaching people this method of Ignatian contemplation that often – by no means always – it is the women who get on very well with it. They can take to this imaginative way of praying with scripture like ducks to water, while those who find the imaginative approach alien or pointless or just plain difficult are often – by no means always – the men. And yet we might expect that women would start from a disadvantage, in that so many of the principal characters in the Bible are men.

What do you do as a woman when you are reading a passage like this one from John's Gospel, where the principal players are all male? Do you assume the role of the silent woman onlooker? Or pretend to be a man? Neither of those is right, of course. You do not restrict yourself to a passive role, when the whole point is to be liberated by the gospel; neither do you put on a pretence when the whole point is to be your real self before God. You do what comes naturally to you. There is nothing wrong with a woman imagining herself as John the Baptist, and she does not need to make a great fuss of picturing herself with a beard and a hairy chest. It is quite unnecessary for a woman to think she is restricted to female characters in the Gospels, for the sex of the character can slip naturally away as the underlying personality comes to the fore. At the same time I should point out that there are some very rich female characters there who repay exploration, like the women who travelled with Jesus (in Luke 8.1-3), including Mary Magdalene, who were probably close witnesses of many miracles and teachings. Or again, it may come more naturally for her to be another character who is not written about but whom she imagines meeting and speaking with Jesus within the context of the events recounted: in other words she can simply be her present self, put into the scene.

Now if I may be a little personal myself, this passage from John is one that has been important to me in my prayer. I have found myself identifying with one of the two disciples who followed Jesus that day. You recall that one is named: 'One of the two who heard John speak, and followed him, was Andrew, Simon Peter's brother.' The other is not named – we are not even told that it was a man – and that has made it easier for me to place myself in that role. Once I have found myself as that disciple, who found Jesus that day, in that way, I have kept the same role through other incidents in the Gospels. I have continued to be that unnamed follower of Jesus, formerly a follower of the Baptist, whose life with Jesus began, at about the tenth hour, by going with him to see where he stayed, and staying with him that day. After that first meeting I am always at his side.

I think this passage is one that is especially valuable for any of us to pray over. Another emphasis in Ignatius' teaching on prayer was to let ourselves get in touch with our deepest desires, with what he calls the *id quod volo* – what I want, what I am looking for. In the Gospel passage Jesus asks the followers – and asks us if we put ourselves in the shoes of those followers – 'what do you seek? what are you looking for?' And the two followers are so confused they cannot think of much of an answer. They know they are following, but are still unsure why. They have no instant complete comprehension of the deep theological significance of John's enigmatic 'Behold the Lamb of God'. They are looking for *something*, of course, but for Jesus? Why they don't even know him yet.

So they reply with another question, 'Rabbi, where are you

staying?' This will enable them to know him, and be with him, and find out more of who he is, and so maybe find out better what it is that they are seeking. By asking them what they are looking for, Jesus has moved them on a step, so that they are asking themselves, 'yes, what am I seeking?', and in their response they are fumbling towards the answer, 'I am seeking to be with you.'

In the same way, at the end of the Fourth Gospel, Jesus asks Mary Magdalene, 'Woman, why are you weeping? Whom do you seek?'. In attempting to answer it – again with another question: 'tell me where you have laid him?' – she suddenly stumbles on a deeper answer. She thought she was looking for a dead body, but she finds she is looking for a living Lord.

So, as we pray, it is good to let Jesus ask us, 'What are you looking for?' And this is a good question with which to end this reflection. Probably we will be caught short, coming from our everyday desires for a good mark in our work or an agreeable companion for our lunch, and not yet reaching our deepest desire for God alone (as Julian of Norwich says: 'God of your goodness give me yourself, for you are enough for me and I may ask nothing that is less, that may be full worship to you. And if I ask anything that is less, I am always wanting – but only in you I have all'). We are caught at the moment when we are beginning to feel our way to a deeper want than we were aware of before, a desire to be with Christ.

So in one way or another, if we pray on this passage, we can say to Jesus through this mystery, 'I want to be with you and see where you are staying and stay with you this day. Then perhaps I will understand better what it is I really want, and understand better who you are, the one with whom I desire to stay.'

Margaret Hebblethwaite

SECOND SIGHT

II Samuel 11.1–12.19; Mark 8.22–26

> The Christ has touched the blind man's eyes,
> But can he really see?
> The cure is not complete, he cries,
> The people look like trees.
> Stay awhile, sweet Jesus,
> Never leave him be:
> Touch his eyes again in love;
> Let the blind man see.

Nathan is angry. He is shaking his fist as he talks. His sons and his brothers are gathered around him, advising him strongly not to carry out his plan. They are telling him not to get involved, that he is playing with fire, that sooner or later, it will rebound on him. They are reminding him that he is a spiritual leader, not a political one. 'Leave politics to the politicians,' they are saying, 'and get on with what you are gifted for. Get on with what God has called you to do.' But their words do not persuade him, nor do they assuage his anger.

The day that made him angry was the day they came and told him that Uriah had disappeared, and that Uriah's widow would be married by the king. Nathan had not known Uriah personally, but he had heard of him from several sources. This Uriah was a poor man, with a humble, but honourable position in the army. He had nothing much to call his own, except his wife, his dignity and his love of the Law. The day they came and told Nathan that Uriah had disappeared was the day the prophet realized that what they had been telling him was true.

Before that, nothing seemed to make him angry. He was at the pinnacle of his career: he was prophet to the Palace. He had the job of walking the palace corridors, talking to those he met, and forging relationships with court officials. Most of all, he had the job of being available to the King, should the great man at any time require a consultation. As prophet to the King, Nathan saw his role as one of proclaiming the love of God for his majesty as for all the people, and of encouraging the royal spiritual life. The prophet had begun to sense how worldly the nation was becoming, and was intent upon revitalizing the people's spirituality – starting at the very top.

But when he heard that Uriah was dead and that the King would marry his widow, it was as if something inside him snapped. He knew that he could not go on the same way as before. People had been murmuring to him since his appointment that there was corruption in the corridors of power, that they had ways of getting rid of people. But he had always refused to see it. 'Leave politics to the politicians', he had thought. But now his eyes had been opened.

But his sons and his brothers are advising him against making this stand. 'It is too dangerous', they are saying. 'We love you. For our sakes, for the sake of all your family, do not endanger your life.' But Nathan's anger will not evaporate. Uriah can be only one of many men who are falling victim to the corruption of the Palace. The prophet can no longer stand back and witness in silence the dispossession and the murder of the poor. Unless someone is prepared to voice the protest, this oppression will continue.

Yes, Nathan knows that the path he takes is dangerous. But now that he has seen, he can no longer hold his peace.

> The Christ has touched the blind man's eyes,
> But can he really see?
> The cure is not complete, he cries,
> The people look like trees.
> Stay awhile, sweet Jesus,
> Never leave him be.
> Touch his eyes again in love.
> Let the blind man see.

David has granted Nathan audience. Not that it is really surprising. Nathan is David's trusted prophet, and the King often turns to him for advice.

Nathan raises an issue which he thinks demands the King's closest attention. A man of wealth has committed a serious offence against a poor man. The man of wealth has abused his power, and left the poor man poorer than he was before. He has committed a gratuitous act of theft.

David listens to Nathan with characteristic respect and attention. This King is a passionate man, a man of prayer, and well-versed in the Law. When he hears Nathan's story, he is understandably angry. He recalls how God once stood against the powerful, bringing the people out of slavery in Egypt. He remembers how, according to God's holy Law, theft and covetousness are sins against God and against one's fellow man. So David makes an immediate response. This case of injustice against the poor is blatant. The rich man must be severely punished. Yes, he will see to it that he is punished.

There is a silence. Then Nathan, as if with a sigh of relief, makes his reply. Hearing, David catches his breath, jolted into a painful recognition of a truth that until now has escaped him. Suddenly he sees himself as he thinks God must see him. He has abused his power and sinned against Uriah, Uriah the poor man, Uriah his subject, Uriah his fellow-sharer in the promised land. He has stolen what was rightfully Uriah's, then taken Uriah's life to simplify the consequences.

And he begins to understand something else about himself. He has been ready to see the injustice of another. He has been ready to judge and punish. Seeing the injustice carried out by another is relatively easy. But understanding that he himself is on the side of the unjust one – that is an insight which has demanded the special Word, the special touch, from God.

Suddenly David sees himself as he believes God must see him, and before Nathan, he confesses his sin against God and against Uriah, and lays himself open to the judgment.

> The Christ has touched the blind man's eyes,
> But can he really see?
> The cure is not complete, he cries,
> The people look like trees.
> Stay awhile, sweet Jesus,
> Never leave him be.
> Touch his eyes again in love;
> Let the blind man see.

Bathsheba is nursing her child. He is five days old, a tiny bundle.

She is pressing him to her breast, encouraging him to suckle. He is pale and sickly, and if he does not suckle, he will die.

She never thought that she would have loved this child so much, this child born of terror and tragedy. She cradles him, smiles into his tiny face, whispering her story to him. Once upon a time, she tells him, his mother was living in the poor part of the city. She was married to a poor man. He was a soldier, and often had to be away from home.

Then one night that she was on her own, two men burst into the house. Before she had had time to react, one of them had seized her, and was pressing his hand over her mouth, so that her terrified scream might not escape. Then the other was coming towards her, breathing into her face, and running a finger down her thigh. 'We *are* in high favour, aren't we?' he was menacing. 'His majesty desires our company. And we couldn't disappoint his majesty, now, could we?' They would be delighted, he said, to escort her to the Palace. But she must be careful to be quiet. She wouldn't like to draw attention to herself, would she? She wouldn't want to embarrass the King and jeopardize her husband's safety.

Thank God, it did not last long. She stood before the King, trembling. He commanded her to take off her clothes, slowly, slowly, one by one, and watched her as she did so, following her every movement, devouring her naked body with his eyes. Then he was pressing himself into her and she was praying, praying that soon it would be over, and that soon she would be free to leave ... No, she never thought that she would have loved this child so much. She presses her baby to her breast, hoping that he will suckle.

Now she lives in the Palace. She is a wife to the King. She is a woman with an important task to perform, a woman appointed to give pleasure to the King, a woman appointed to bear sons to the King. When the days of her purification are complete, she will have to lie with him again. Then it will be her duty to open herself to him again, again and again, as often as it takes for him to tire of her, or for her to conceive once more. And she will pray to God to let her conceive quickly, this very time, this very night, so that she may be spared any more brutish nights, so that she may rest while another woman takes her place.

There is no going back. At least the marriage to the King has saved her from the poverty and the ignominy of widowhood. What would she have done, a widow, pregnant in the poor part of the city? Yet the riches and the finery to which she has acceded will never console her. She cannot but compare them to the simplicity from which she came. And she has no news of her family, no word of her friends. They belong now to a distant, foreign world, a world she must forget or forever grieve over. But Uriah she will never forget. She will never forget the life she had with him. She will never forget his words of gentleness, his honesty, his soft caresses. She will always grieve for her husband. And sometimes, when the anger and the pain grow too strong to bear, she clutches the infant to her. Out of all of this, this little one is all she has left. Nothing must be allowed to take him from her now.

She never thought that she would love this child so much. He is five days old, a tiny bundle. Bathsheba presses him to her, encouraging him to take her breast. He is pale and sickly, and if he does not suckle, he will die.

The Christ has touched our blinded eyes,
But can we really see?
The cure is not complete, we cry,
The people look like trees.
Stay awhile, sweet Jesus,
Never leave us be.
Touch our eyes again in love.
Help us all to see.

Mary Cotes

TRUE VINE

The two families planted a vine and a fig tree to mark our betrothal.

The vine was a spur from the great vine which supplied most of the wine for our household. This vine was so old that its stem stood without any support like the trunk of an aged tree. Every year my father would pace around it sighing and talk of digging it up to replace it with new stock. But every year the great vine continued to bear more than all the other vines. The shoot they planted for us was the first to break from its lifeless tresses in the springtime of our betrothal year. It grew from wood everyone knew should have been thrown on the fire many years before. Before I was even born.

The fig tree was the blessing of Jousef's family upon our marriage. They joked and said that its tiny green embryo figs would be replaced by a fine harvest in a few years time. Then it would be time, they told us, when we would reap a harvest of our own. 'Look at the child. There's a bellyfull of fine green figs in there. She just needs a couple of summers for the ripening.'

Although you are a stranger you have heard perhaps that they burn the houses? If the children throw stones at the soldiers in the street, if a dog so much as yaps at the heels of one of those plump foreign boys that walk our streets, then with a quick and casual fury they drive a family from its home. They break the furniture, they smear the whitewashed walls with filth and then they put the ravaged house to the torch.

I think you might not know that they also wring the necks of the chickens and slit the bellies of the dogs and carry away the goats. Perhaps you did not know that they tear up the mint and the dill and the fennel and put an axe to the olive tree, to the fig and to the vine. A house can be built again in a month. You can have chickens and puppies in the yard within a season and green plants spring up again at the first sowing. It takes many years for olives, vines and figs to flourish. If the human stock is cut down it cannot be replaced.

When two of their boys walking our streets were ambushed, one killed and the other beaten, many homes were raised. They cut down the great vine then and as its long tresses cracked to the axe I felt all my father's strength break with it. Its wood shows no signs that sap had flowed within it for years. It burnt as fiercely and brightly as dead wood burns but we know that this 'dead wood' had produced always the biggest harvest.

They did not take an axe to our fig tree. It was too small for that. It only took a soldier's one hand to tear it up with its roots. The dormant rod of our vine they left. It looked just like a bent twig in the shelter of the wall. I don't think they noticed it even, they were in such a hurry raising our building and our planting so that there would be no hiding place left. When all was cleared Jousef's brother could be seen standing. He had been with those who had made the ambush in the darkness. They killed him in the sunlight and left his body amongst the rubble; the drying roots to which a few stones clung suspended.

Jousef was beautiful. Deep sorrow added to his beauty. Jousef was the most beautiful boy in the village.

Beauty is not always loved.

I remember when we were very young and the waistcloth which he wore hid nothing of his body from the eye. Other children treated him with shyness. Children watched Jousef but they did not seek his company and children's cunning prevented them from wishing to walk next to him in the street. I saw this myself that he was often alone.

Of course his mother loved him – but she loved the others more. She cried when her daughters were betrothed and those were tears of loss not joy. She wept when Jousef's brother took a wife; tasting the salt she would taste again when she saw his body laid out where the fields had turned to dust. Amongst the ashes.

She did not cry at our betrothal. She made honey cakes and said how fine it was to see a son prepare to leave his mother's keeping. She was relieved she had spent her one golden coin and could feel rich again with her fortune that was nothing more than a fistfull of small change.

Well I am glad that there were no tears at our betrothal. I am glad that people danced and were happy then and did not think of the sadness the future might bring. And I am glad that I took in my hand the golden hand of Jousef. Jousef who was the most beautiful boy in the village and who I loved.

Oh I remember. I am just a girl but I watch for him. He is one year older than I am and sometimes we play together. Jousef is beautiful and when I close my eyes he is still beautiful. He smells of vanilla pods. He sounds like cool water poured from a damp clay jar. And then they are making plans for our promising. So we, who have been so familiar, I remember a small boy whose waist cloth hid nothing of his body from the eyes, we became mysterious to each other. Already I feel him growing inside me. My body reaches out when I pass him in the street but I look away with my eyes and we do not speak.

Jousef will be mine and he is preparing himself for our wedding. When he was a child and the soldiers fired a house Jousef always cried. He cried when he heard though the people were not kin to him or even friendly with his parents. After he had cried Jousef would take clay from the river and make new pots for cooking. When he was older he would take his knife and carve fine wooden bowls for the homeless children. Now he is strong and almost grown he takes axe and saw and cuts new timber to rebuild a charred roof. He makes a new strong door. He carves the secret patterns on the chest that each girl needs to fill with the things she must have as she becomes a woman. Jousef's brother was cut down and from that day Jousef has become a carpenter. When he is not working for others he is choosing the timbers; he is measuring the foundations; he is building a fine house for us.

I am willing but I am not eager. I know what it means to become a woman and so knowing I am not eager. I feel my time is fast passing and my hour has almost come and so I am up early in the morning. Away before they can hand me the ring of plaited grass to balance the heavy water jug upon my head. I am throwing bones in the market place with the other children. I am shaking the tambourine as we make our wedding dances, I am sounding the slow drum as we mark our own funerals in solemn procession.

Late back at night I sit amongst the puppies on the dark side of the fire. Let them forget me. Let them not see in the full light that I am almost grown. She is just a child my sister. Too young for breasts.

But the hour bore down upon me and I could not escape. It was the first warm day of a late spring but I did not go with other children to the terraces to watch the men tie in the first new shoots of the vines. I stayed in the darkness of the house but then it felt as if the walls of our house had been torn down and light was shining all around. The enemy that did this was an angel. The Angel told me what I already knew that my time had come.

You may not understand what I did next. I crossed to the chest where I had begun to store the things I needed to mark my passover to womanhood and I took out a head cloth. The cloth every girl must wear when she becomes a woman to bind her hair, to tame her hair. I put on the scarf, once taken it cannot be removed. The girl is grown.

The Angel had come to show me that my hour had come but I felt that this taking of the scarf ... it was not the wrong thing to do exactly ... it was the only thing to do. But it was not what the bright Angel had come to bring about.

What the Angel sang to me, it was the music of the wedding dance and the funeral march played together, what the angel sang to me was that I who had put from myself the last liberty of childhood had become the bearer of hope. Hope that can only come from those who have lost the taste of freedom; whose homes are torn down; whose fields are destroyed. Hope comes burning down on those whose heads are covered. Only those who are not free can be the bearer of this unnatural thing. How could I shut my ears to the music which had collapsed the walls of my home. How could I close my eyes to the light which had burnt down the walls. I was pregnant from the very moment and not with my strong hands, or my strong desire, could I dislodge the child growing there beneath my loose belt.

When the Angel left and the dark walls enclosed me again I wished for pure grief and weeping but I could not. The sickness was spreading through me. No time for mourning my lost soul only the urgent needs of this body. All my energy focussed in the body. The need to take great gasps of air between the retching, O Jousef, Jousef, it is not your child. Not your gentle hands parting my legs. It is another power which has overshadowed us.

I did not speak with Jousef until the first days of sickness had passed. Then on three evenings we walked together along the terraces. On the first evening he said nothing to me at all. On the second evening he cursed. 'What is wrong with building and planting? What is to be despised in a child conceived in love and raised according to custom? What is unclean about my body? Why does God want all to be cleared away and human hearts salt and barren and dead before from nowhere and nothing a great harvest is given?'

On the third night it is warmer and clearer. He moves closer to me as we walk. I look at him in the moonlight. I remember the lonely face of a small boy whose waist cloth hid nothing of his body from the eyes. I say 'come to me Jousef' I know betrothal can never be celebrated as a wedding now. There is no point in waiting. My breasts are heavy and all my skin is tender. I feel as if I will bruise if I am touched and yet all my desire is to yield. Jousef is beautiful and the deep sorrow has added to his beauty. Jousef has the skilled fingers of a carpenter. But Jousef will not.

He is not a man of hope. Jousef thinks that hope is cruel. Jousef saw his brother cut down for hope. Hope when people are born as we are and die as we do is a curse. It turns all that could be sweet, sour. Jousef is a carpenter. He rebuilds what is broken down and makes the things that people need if our life in this land is to continue. Jousef will not lie with me whilst hope possesses my body.

But Jousef will shelter me and wait to see what can be built up again when this deliverance is passed.

Heather Walton

THREE WISE WOMEN

A *midrash* on Matthew 2.1–12 for Epiphany

Everyone has a story. This is a story told by three women in the way women's stories are told; by sharing and affirming experiences.

We are three women and some have called us wise. Wise with the wisdom of our mothers who were before us. Wise to teach our daughters the ways of the world. Wise to see God and say so. We lived in troubled times and each of us knew pain as well as joy. We kept going, finding support in each other and in The Other, which was more than just a feeling but something rather beyond us.

The first of us was a widow who has had many children; but husband and children were gone and this woman lived on alone. They had all disappeared, as had many others. These events may be repeated in the lives of other women, in other times and other places. This family had just disappeared. Where they had gone wasn't known. Who was responsible? Well, we could all take a reasonable guess at that. Herod and his henchmen probably, trying to clear the country of subversive elements or militant tendencies.

It's not easy for a woman to live with troubled memories. She needs to know where her loved ones are. So this woman searches, follows up leads, keeps looking, asks around; someone must know the answer.

The second was a mystic; one who had dreams, saw signs and visions. Difficult for the patriarchal priesthood of the time to cope with this sort of thing. Well, women are such an emotional lot and if you let one in – where will it all end?

She'd been called some pretty nasty names; witch, whore. She'd even had to move home a few times. But some recognized the words and signs were from God. They came to listen and share. Sometimes the words were strange – held out amazing promises of God's reign of justice, peace and harmony in all creation. In the temple, dry old men dismissed them, but someone must know the answer.

The third woman was a midwife. She'd had a child herself, many years ago – dead almost before breathing life and those had been painful days. But the knowledge of healing had continued to grow and had been shared between more women. It was life-giving and life sustaining and many had been born and thrived on it. It had helped those who wanted children, and those who didn't, those with sick or handicapped children and those who needed healing and wholeness for themselves and their families. It hadn't always been understood, some were very suspicious of it; but someone must know the answer.

The rhythms of life had ebbed and flowed through the years and had brought us together as we looked for an answer. In the end we were more or less catapulted into the moment. One with news of the lost family; just a faint possibility but worth following up. One needing to move on again, unconventionality breeds suspicion, it's better to be on the road. One hearing through the sister of a sister about a young woman facing childbirth many miles from home. So we set out. A funny sort of journey though. You see there was this light. No one else seemed to notice it really and we didn't think we'd seen it before. But it was there with us and it never seemed to go out.

We found ourselves at the royal court – not the route we had intended to take. We weren't very welcome there either. There seemed to be no answers to our enormous questions in these tiny minds. Someone must know the answer. The light hadn't gone out. Perhaps that was a sign. We stayed on the road and kept looking.

When we got there we could hardly believe it. Yet, at the same time, we all knew we had arrived. It was a sort of shed, a lean-to beside an inn. It had animals and straw in it. There was a young woman and a man with her, who both made us very welcome. 'You'll have come to see the baby' she said and we all agreed that we had. We'd come all that way just for that; to see a baby. It seems that many others had come too, each with their own questions. All of them ordinary people just like us.

We looked at the baby. Babies are quite amazing aren't they? Sucking quietly at the woman's breast, a perfect part of God's creation. We were lost for a while just wondering at it all.

The the first one, the widow, she said: 'It takes a lot of money to bring up a family these days. I can see that you don't have much (the couple exchanged a glance). Here, take this, it may be small but it is gold. It was a part of my dowry, when I married. It may keep you going for a bit or come in handy for emergencies.' She laid the piece of gold in the woman's hand and it seemed to light the faces of both mother and baby.

The second said: 'This is a strange sight, I hardly know what to say. A baby in an animal shed. It doesn't smell that good either. Here, I have a little incense. Burn it to sweeten the air.' The fragrance mingled with the straw and the animals and seemed to help everyone feel at home.

The third said:

'I'm worried about the possible health risks. I mean, it does seem very crowded in this town. It's very difficult to get clean water. This little one is vulnerable and so is the mother. Take this myrrh; it'll be useful to clean things up, purify them.' It was an important thought as that family had a lot of growing to do on the road between life and death.

The mother accepted all the gifts graciously; grateful for the generosity and spontaneity of the occasion. We three left and on the way back, avoiding the royal court and its dubious occupant, we thought about it all.

Someone had to have the answer to the whereabouts of a family suddenly disappeared. But the weight of grief had been given up when the gold had been given away. A new family of concerns had been adopted. The questions hadn't gone away but justice was worth struggling for.

Someone must have the answer to interpret words, dreams and signs. But the breath of the incense mingling with the smells of the earth said the signs are all around you and the vision has just begun. The questions hadn't gone away but peace was worth speaking out for.

Someone must have the answer to the gift of life and death; babies and mothers struggling with hygiene, disease and poverty. But the purity of the love shown in the faces of that young family reflected a promise that would be with us all, up to the very gates of death and beyond. The questions hadn't gone away but the fullness of creation and the love working in it was a promise that touched us all.

We went home. Three ordinary women. We lived our lives. Some called us wise because of the way we tried to answer many questions. We think it would be more honest to say we were amazed. The three amazed women. For we were amazed that we should see God. But we did and we're not afraid to say so.

Janet Lees

CREATION

Once a woman found herself in a beautiful field. It was early spring and the day had just begun. She moved through the grass, her feet were bare and new life filled her body. She could feel life kick within her. The woman smiled and said to the God whose name was love,

'This place is surely where I must have my child.'

But said the God,

'Daughter, you have not seen enough of our world
yet, you must walk further.'

So the woman walked on. She saw a golden flower in the green grass and bent down to know its scent. A passer-by said

'It's no use smelling a crocus. They have no perfume'
'Oh but they do!' said the woman,
'They smell of the damp warm earth where life is cradled and the smell is very good.'

Feeling happy because of the knowledge of life in her heart and the movement of life in her body she walked on. She came to a house where a father played with his child in the garden. In his hand he held a cup of soapy water and he was blowing bubbles into the spring air. She watched as the child chased the bubbles full of wonder and joy. She saw with the child's eyes that the bubbles contained all the colours of the rainbow in their tiny spheres.

She said to the God whose name was love

'Truly, the brightly coloured circle of the earth is a wonderful place.'
'Walk on my daughter and see more', God answered her.

The day had passed its mid point and the sun was fading. She began to feel cold. The path she had taken through the fields was paved now, then it became a road. The lights of a town were beckoning in the distance. It looked inviting.

But when she reached the city the windows and doors of the houses were locked and closed against her. She began to feel afraid. The night was cold and she had no place to go. Then she saw, in the heart of the city, a large building enclosed with huge walls and guarded with a great iron gate.

'This must have been built for safety and refuge' she thought. 'It will be a warm, dark sanctuary waiting for life to grow within it. It will be a good place to have my child.'

She followed a man in dark grey clothes into the building. He had a bunch of keys and she kept close by him as he walked through corridors, barred by iron doors, and peered through spy holes into cells with iron bars at the windows.

'This is the city within the city' she thought.
'Surely the world is a hard cold place of iron and stone.'

What she saw as she followed the man filled her with sadness. In one cell sat three men, their heads in their hands. She was sickened by the smell that came from the bucket that was their communal lavatory. In another cell stood a woman naked, waiting to be searched by cold inquiring hands. In a small dark room a young man hung from the ceiling by a rope of knotted blankets. He was dead. His face was contoured in appalling pain. His agony racked her body and she felt his pain provoke a travail inside her. In distress she screamed to the God whose name was love.

'Take me from this evil place. I cannot bear my child here'.
'Where would you like to go my daughter?'

In that cold, evil-smelling house of death she thought of sunshine, water, waves, the sea.

'Life comes from the sea.'

She said 'take me where there is warmth, a sand beach and sweet water in which the fish swim and from which the birds feed'.

As she spoke the woman felt herself lifted up and carried away to rest in a gentle place where the sea murmured and her body was warmed by the sun. Anxiously she waited to see if she could still feel new life kept safe in her body. The child kicked hard and strong within and relief flooded through her. Her precious child had survived the ordeal. Exhausted she fell asleep in the sand.

When she awoke the sun still caressed her. She stretched out feeling her strength had returned.

'This must be the right place to have my child' she said to the God whose name was love.
'Look around my daughter, look around' the God replied.

So the woman looked, and she saw fishing boats pulled high above the water line. She saw the sea black with oil, dead fish and dead birds washed to the shore. She looked harder and saw the sad eyes of the people who lived by the sea. People who could no longer fish for food to feed themselves or to sell in the market place. She saw children with empty eyes and empty stomachs. What could she do? How could she help?

'What have you done to these people. How could you allow this to happen. Don't you see the people dying. The birds and fish, the sea itself is black with oil. Life is choked at its source. Meanwhile you do nothing you just watch everything die.'
'Daughter'
said the God
'Where shall I take you?'

The woman's body was all pain now. The travail of the sea people one with her own travail. But the pain of her body was nothing compared to the pain confusion that filled her mind. Who was this God whose name she had thought was love? Was the love for her and not for all? Could it be for her child and not all the children? Could she let herself be removed from this place to give birth if other children were born and died here.

'I shall stay and let my baby be born amongst the other lost children. I won't leave this place with you. Better my baby die than live in comfort whilst others suffer' she said.
'Then welcome into my embrace' said the God whose name was love.
'You come close to my heart when you share in this sorrow. My sorrow.'

And the woman looked on the face of the God whose name was

love and recognized her as the midwife who would groan and push with her as she gave birth. Recognized her as someone who had shared many a long labour.

And the woman, whose name was Creation, trusted her pain to the God whose name was love who would deliver her.

As we, trusting in God and in one another, shall give birth from our weeping to the new life that shall redeem us all.

Hazel Walton

BAD FRIDAY

A sermon for Good Friday

I have a bit of a problem with this story. It's not really like some of the other stories about my somewhat tiresome guardian angel. For one thing it happened in the night.

Oddly enough – well it does seem odd to me – my guardian angel does not often appear in the night. As a matter of fact, I strongly suspect that this is because she has such a pathetic imagination. She can't cope with dreams, and is confined to the daily. You read in the Bible of truly wonderful dreams; like Jacob's ladder or Joseph putting his brothers in their place by boasting about their measly little sheaves of corn bowing down to his great big fat one.

I think a few dreams would be fun, and a much better way of getting spiritual guidance because you could chat for hours with your friends about interpretations and Freud and sex and things. But do I dream? No, I don't. All I get are her clichés, and her interfering pettiness, and her tedious scruples.

Of course, she doesn't agree. She says the reason that I don't get dreams is because I sleep so soundly, for which – in her opinion – I ought to be grateful. I find this terribly unromantic, but it's true: frankly the minute I turn the light out I slump asleep and practically never wake up again until the alarm clock rings. But you might well think a half-way competent angel would be able to deal with such a minor impediment. It makes you wonder. If I were God the very least I'd do is check that all the guardian angels had *some* creative flair, and ones like mine who are so totally prosaic and mundane would be kept in heaven, well out of the way of delicate and aspiring souls.

Anyway, all this is pretty irrelevent because as it happens this story did take place in the night. At twelve minutes past three to be precise. The very worst imaginable time to be woken up by an angel with a slightly common accent manifesting herself all of a sudden, and saying,

'I've just popped in to say good-bye.'

'Go away,' I muttered. In my own defence I must stress that I was nine-tenths asleep. Then I remembered with a horrid jerk that I had said much the same thing to my daughter one night when she was ten years old and had been woken up two hours later by my very angry oldest son reporting that she was retching and shivering and swallowing her pain in the bathroom, and telling him not to wake me or I would be cross. She had acute appendicitis; and had been wheeled into surgery still apologizing for having disturbed me.

(By the way, in fairness since I am always complaining about Angel, I should mention that she was completely marvellous that night, and came with us all the way in the ambulance and did try to comfort me, and reassure me that I could go on being a mother. Unlike usual, she didn't rub my face in guilt. I refused her consolation though – I knew all about my inadequacy and awfulness on that occasion.)

So with that unfortunate precedent looming in my consciousness I sat up and said, 'Sorry, Angel, I was asleep. Is it something important?'

'I just popped in to say good-bye.'
'Can't that wait?' I asked peevishly.

'You are always telling me you want divine revelations in the cold small hours of the night,' she said. If anyone else had used that tone to me I would have thought they were being a bit sarcastic, but Angel is too dense for such subtleties.

'I don't see your departure exactly as a spiritual revelation,' I muttered. And then it hit me. Her departure. She couldn't leave me, not just like that. I hadn't been *that* nasty to her; it was just that we disagreed about quite a lot of things. Surely angels could accept and tolerate difference? Surely she wouldn't be that small minded? What did she expect, slavish obedience or something? Not that I minded of course; if she wanted to desert her god-given duties, that was up to her; it was none of my business. It was just the principle of the thing.

'Angel ...' I began.

'You know we always take this Friday off,' she said.

She always did too. Regular as clock-work. 'Fine,' I said, ignoring a great surge of relief and happiness, 'I don't see why you had to wake me up for that. Did you think I'd forget or something? See you Easter Day.'

There was a pause. Then she said, with what sounded like an unusual degree of diffidence, 'I thought I'd better remind you about fasting.'

'Fasting! For Good Friday!' I exclaimed, 'Oh don't be so antiquated. No one does that anymore.'

She didn't argue with me, there was just one of her long silences.

'I'm not,' I said boldly, 'into all that body-hating, masochistic, mediaeval stuff. Do you fast in heaven?'

Her silence continued. I waited hopefully. For once, I thought, I had her where I wanted her. In the wrong. After a bit I heard her sniffle; the poor thing was probably embarrassed. I felt a moment of compassion, but, thinking about all the times she had forced me to apologize, I clung to my moment of triumph.

'Well,' I said, after I thought she had been silent for long enough, 'do you fast in heaven?'

The silence went on a bit longer. It was almost beginning to feel awkward, then she said, quite suddenly and almost crossly for her,

'Well we can't, can we? We don't eat. We don't feel hunger.'

But the odd thing was that she didn't sound the least bit pleased with herself – either for her minor victory over me, or for this abundant proof of the superiority of angels.

We fell into silence again. It went on for a long time. I thought she had finished harrassing me and would dematerialize herself in her own good time, so I lay down again and tried to go back to sleep. She was still there, hovering in my left cortex as only angels can. Now and again she made a funny snuffly sound, as though she had a cold; but when someone has just reminded you, and in rather a disagreeable tone, that they don't experience hunger, you can't very well offer them a handkerchief and tell them to blow their nose.

It was all very annoying. I felt more and more obstinate. She could stay or go in her own good time, but I was not going to initiate another conversation. It was three o'clock in the morning, for goodness sake, and no time for a busy woman to be having to deal with sulky angels. And in passing I would like to say that no human being, not even the adolescent male, can sulk as efficiently and thoroughly as your average angel. All I wanted was to go back to sleep.

The snuffling, however, did not diminish. On the contrary. Then I realized that she was crying. I mean really crying. It was a bit embarrassing actually, like the first time a grown-up man cries those terrible awkward male tears on to you; you know it's a sort of compliment, you have an inkling of how much they need to do it, and, at the same time, you just wish they wouldn't, because they are so bad at it. Angel's tears made me squirm a bit; I nearly asked her how it was that angels could cry when they couldn't eat, and then decided that would not be very kind. But I really did feel quite strongly that it was an angel's rôle to comfort not to be comforted, so I let her get on with it for a bit.

In the end it got to me; that irrepressable maternal instinct – or since I'm a feminist perhaps I should say human instinct – that simply prevents you from letting a person, or I suppose an angel for that matter, cry. I wasn't best pleased about it.

'Oh for heaven's sake, Angel,' I said, when I could bear it no longer, 'Whatever's the matter now?'
But she didn't reply. She just went on crying. It was really getting on my nerves. I said,
'All right then, if it means that much to you I will fast today.'
You might think that this generosity of spirit would cheer anyone up, but it didn't work with her.
'Please.' I could hear myself begging. When I think of all the times that she has felt free to interupt me and demand that I talk to her about whatever idiotic banality she chooses. And now she

was refusing me the same privilege. It wasn't fair. That sounded a
bit childish, so I changed my mind. It was outrageous!

'You're behaving like a teenager,' I said; I tried to say it firmly
rather than angrily. Three teenage children in one household is
quite enough, without having to put up with a teenaged spiritual
force that skulked about somewhere slightly above my top
vertebra. Once my daughter locked herself in the bathroom and
howled for three hours, and when she finally came out she
demanded cinnamon toast and refused point blank ever to say
what the matter was. I was not going through that again,
especially not with a blasted angel about whom I could not even
have the dubious satisfaction of murmering 'boy-friend-trouble'
with the world-weariness of middle age.

'Angel,' I said, 'don't be such a baby.' But when babies cry you
can comfort them. You can kiss them and cuddle them; you can
wrap them warm and safe against you, petting their pink, flushed
faces. You can find their favourite teddy-bear, its face already
worn bald with the receiving of love and the giving of furry
comfort. You cannot do any of these things, or anything like
them, with an angel. Grey matter may be soft and warm, but
cuddly it is not. I reached through my mind and spirit for
tenderness and comfort and found my hands empty. It was very
frustrating.

The crying went on and on. I had tried emotional bribery and I
had tried emotional blackmail. There was nothing left except
love. And, given the difficulties of our relationship, and the
degree to which I felt irritated by her, it was not an easy thing to
offer.

'Angel,' I said, as carefully as I knew how. 'I love you. When
you came to say good-bye I had forgotten about the Friday bank
holiday or whatever you call it in heaven, and I thought you were
leaving me permanently. I was sad. I didn't even know I was sad,
but I was. I was sad because I love you. And because I need you.
But honestly I would rather you left me if that made you happier
than have you stay like this.'

I felt a complete idiot when I said this. There are many things
you find yourself doing as you get older which your optimistic
young self would never have known how to dream of, but very
high on that list for me comes sitting up in bed at four in the

morning, in a flannel nightie, trying to tell *anyone*, let alone a weeping and unresponsive citizen of heaven, that you love her.

But it worked. Not magically or instantaneously or anything, but the solid flow of desolate tears turned back into the infuriating adenoidal snuffles, and then into the hiccups of a sob-exhausted toddler.

Finally she said, 'It's worse than you know.'

'What is?' I asked, relieved that we were getting somewhere, but weary with the strain.

'I'm jealous.'

'Jealous!' I exclaimed startled. 'Jealous?' I inquired in an attempt at non-judgmental open-minded interest.

There was a bit more snuffling, and then finally she said, 'I'm jealous of *you*.'

'Me?' I said tentatively, though really I meant 'what on earth are you talking about?'

'Yes you. I'm jealous of you because you can get hungry. Because you can get hurt, I mean physically hurt, because you can have pain, and suffering, and agony.'

'But that's not nice. I mean, those things aren't nice. They're horrid. Why does that make you jealous?'

'Because you can be with Him today and we can't. We just can't. We tried and tried and we couldn't understand. After the Last Supper he went away from us. We thought we could rescue him and he wouldn't let us. Then we thought at least we could comfort him, and we couldn't. That peasant woman could; she may be the Queen of Heaven now, but then she was just a middle-aged woman from the sticks, but she could comfort him, and her half-daft fisherman friend and that red-headed whore from Magdala; they could comfort him because they could understand. And we, the first born of the creation, the spinners of the seven spheres, the messengers of the Holy Spirit, the powers and dominions, cherubim and seraphim, angels and archangels; we could do nothing. He didn't need us. We could not go where he had gone. We could not understand. That's why we all take the day off; not for a holiday but because we know we're useless.

They scourged him and we could not feel it. They crowned him with thorns and it didn't hurt us. They banged those nails through his hands and we wept for his humiliation, but we could not go where he had gone when he went into the pain-place whatever that is. He gave you the glory, the privilege of going where he went, into the body in all its beauty and holiness, into the pain and the pleasure of the flesh. He loves you more than he loves us. And you take that privilege, that gift, that joy, so lightly that you don't even care enough to fast once a year. *Of course I'm jealous.*'

She began to cry again. So did I, as a matter of fact. We wept together and we could not comfort each other.

'We don't call it Good Friday,' she gulped after a while, 'we call it Bad Friday.'

'Angel,' I said, 'I really will fast today. I'll fast for me and I'll fast for you.' This time the generosity of spirit was slightly more authentic.

'Thank you,' she said.

It was nearly dawn, grey light was coming through the curtains. She got ready to depart. I began to think about how impressed my children would be when they saw I wasn't eating, not even the hot-crossed buns. It might even reconvert my middle son who was trying out existentialism at that moment. I might even become a great ascetic saint pretty soon, known for the rigours of my life and for my charity to lesser mortals.

Angel put a stop to that; she paused in her soft descent through my cranial cavity, and murmered,

'Watch it, sister; we haven't even started on hair-shirts and flagellation yet, and they're tough.' But she was grinning a shy, happy, little grin.

'Peace be with you,' she said as usual, 'and see you on Sunday.'

Sara Maitland

EATING THE FRUIT

The 'text' for this sermon comes not from the Bible, but from the television: Jeanette Winterson's screen adaptation of her own novel, *Oranges are not the Only Fruit*.[1] The particular scene I have in mind is one of exorcism. Jess, a young woman in love with another young woman, is imprisoned at home by three women (including her mother). The three are leading 'ladies' in the pentecostal Lancashire church of which Jess has been a faithful member since early childhood. In command of the operation is the pastor (male), who ties her up with the so-called 'cords of love'. He sits astride Jess's body and pins her, face down, to the floor, pulling her head back almost to the point of asphyxiation. He gags her with a handkerchief and exhorts her to, 'Think about Jesus ... his goodness and his loving kindness ... not soft bodies and easy pleasure, but the virtues of your saviour. Think about the crucified Christ, and his sacrifice for you.'

Jess and Melanie are being punished for being best friends and lovers. They experience their love as wholesome and good. Where they had known loneliness and boredom, they now know intimacy, closeness and excitement. They even theologize about it, likening themselves to David and Jonathan in the Bible: 'although they were married, they loved each other best ... and when we're married, we'll love each other best.' Given her background, Jess hears frequent references to sexual immorality and 'unnatural passions', but she sees no connection between the 'evil' which is often condemned in this way and the love she experiences. Indeed, after making love with Melanie, she whispers, 'This *can't be* unnatural passions, can it?'.

That's the background. Now I'd like to explore the cocktail of Christianity, violence and sexuality which make this scene so compelling and, I believe, instructive for a consideration of the experience of women within the church.

The first point to notice is that Jess's interpretation of her experience counts for nothing. Her feelings are misrepresented and denied. What she calls love, her church calls perversion, and will not be persuaded otherwise. When Jess and Melanie are confronted by the pastor with their 'sick and sinful' behaviour; when he accuses them of 'falling foul of their lusts', Jess retaliates. 'It's not like that' she protests, and there ensues a familiar battle over biblical interpretation. Predictably, the pastor quotes Saint Paul: '... therefore God gave them up to the lusts of their hearts, to the dishonouring of their bodies ... the women exchanged natural relations for unnatural ...' But Jess interrupts, 'Paul also says in Romans 14 that nothing is unnatural in itself. It is made unnatural by those who think it is unnatural.' She is intelligent, quick, strong and eloquent. Her knowledge of the Bible is faultless. Even so, she doesn't stand a chance. She has flown in the face of an institution that renders her powerless. In the short term, she is faced with four adults and lacks the physical strength to withstand them, and even if she had that, she would lack the economic independence to leave. In the long-term, she lacks the power of definition for her point of view to prevail. She lies pinned to the floor for three days and three nights, having no choice. Later in life, she leaves the institution, having no choice.

Many women will recognize this scenario. Lesbians within the church lack the power of self-definition. We are profoundly and routinely insulted by a theology which explains away our intimate relationships and our identities as the result of 'childhood psychological damage', and by a moral superiority which says we are making the best of a situation which is 'intrinsically flawed'. Similarly, heterosexual women who enjoy close and significant relationships outside of marriage have these relationships trivialized when they are labelled 'trial marriages', or apostatized when they are labelled 'adulterous'. We know, however, that in reality we 'love well' in comparison to many of those who condemn us. Their attitudes constitute a violation of our identity and of our right to name ourselves. Like Jess, however, there is little we can do except remove ourselves from the firing line. No matter how loud our voices, how well-versed our theological critique, and how determined our political activity, institutional change happens at a pace determined by the powerful, and it usually takes a man to say once what a woman has said one thousand times, before our experience is heard.

Before we despair at the invulnerability of theological orthodoxy, we should notice that there is a sense in which it is also extremely fragile. For Jess, as for so many others, *falling in love* brings the whole edifice crashing down. Her experience no longer 'fits' the tradition she has inherited and it is the latter which immediately loses all sense and meaning. Like the proverbial salt, it has lost its taste, and the church's vain attempt forcibly to restore it would be laughable were it not so vicious. In the face of the resulting violence, Jess's only option is to leave the institution which threatens to destroy her. Like running away from home for survival, this is not easy, for she faces the loss of all that has hitherto made sense of her life and given it structure. The task ahead is the re-creation of meaning in the absence of what had been her primary community of reference.

Notice that Jess is not punished, but exorcized. This brings us to a second important point. The ultimate insult is not that Jess's experience is considered wrong – disordered – but that she is deprived even of the right to *own* her feelings; to be a moral agent. She is apparently in the grip of an external force and has done 'wrong' because she is colonized by demons. And for those who think exorcism is a million miles away from their own experience – liberal Christianity has a less dramatic equivalent in the 'sympathy' and 'compassion' it extends to lesbians, who are considered to be morally deficient through no fault of our own. Whether devil-possessed or sick – lesbians 'can't help it'. The cure is supposedly complete surrender to God. The ideal is to become nothing but passive vessels through which God can work out his purpose.

This is not the kind of theology most women need. Feminist theologians have pointed out that a theology of self-annihilation is a solution to a male problem – too strong a sense of self. But women are already constructed to live through others – to deny ourselves. In its inappropriateness, traditional theology ranks alongside the pastor's exhortation to Jess, to 'think about the crucified Christ' in the midst of her own 'crucifixion'. When Christianity preaches self-abnegation to women, it consolidates our 'victim' status. This is graphically illustrated in *Christianity and Incest*,[2] a study of women abused as children within Christian families. Not one of the ten women whose stories appear in that book had learned that self love was important. On the contrary, they had learned that it was wrong to stand up for themselves. In a world where women are routinely subjected to physical and sexual violence, and where the fight for control over our own bodies and our own fertility is seemingly never won, we should be wary of the implications of a theology which preaches that our bodies and our actions are not our own.

Although both men and women are encouraged to give themselves up to the will of God, the expectation is that only men stand a chance of being successful. In the story, the pastor claims for himself the voice of God, thus obscuring the fact that *he* is doing what he is doing. As far as he is concerned, it is not he who acts, but God who acts through him. Similarly, when so-called men-of-God argue against – to take one example – the ordination of women, they do so on the grounds that *God* says it's forbidden, or that *God* thinks it's an abomination. Sad though it may be to exclude women from the priesthood, they say, the fault lies with God, not with men. Male theology allows men to abdicate responsibility for their own beliefs.

For me the final lesson to be drawn from Jess's experience is a political one: that the power of patriarchy is more subtle than the straightforward domination of women by men. It is significant that three women take charge of Jess's exorcism once the pastor has set it in train. There is a horizontal violence that comes into play when some women are given a little power so that the majority of women may have even less. Those who are allowed power tend to be those who can be relied upon to reflect and echo establishment values. No one should be surprised that the women who oppose women's ordination attract a higher profile than women who favour it. Neither should we be surprised that such women exist at all. The dominant ideologies of sexism, racism and heterosexism are instilled with equal vigour into all of us. Women are disadvantaged as a result of sexism, so it tends to be women who work to overthrow it. But there is nothing essential about being a woman which means one automatically shares the feminist agenda, just as there is nothing essential about men which means they will oppose it.

In conclusion, Jess's experience of violence in a Christian context may be extreme, but it is not unusual. Hundreds of women have felt it necessary to escape physical, emotional, spiritual and sexual violence by walking away from institutional Christianity, often after long and painful engagements with it. And there are hundreds more on the brink of counting ourselves among them. This is not escapism. Often it is the only way for women to *opt in* to that which is life-affirming and creative. The biggest mistake we – and those within the institution – can make is to assume that these women cease to make a difference. Church policies are shaped by their absence as they are by their presence.

The silence which falls upon the world that has been left behind is matched by louder calls for justice from those who remain. Meanwhile, the option is open for those women who have taken leave of the institutional church to seek to get on with *being church* in a more authentic way, elsewhere.

[1] *Oranges are not the Only Fruit* (1985) Vintage Books 1992; *Oranges are not the Only Fruit*, Television Script, BBC Television; Vintage Books 1994.

[2] Annie Imbers-Fransen and Ineke Jonker-de Putter, *Christianity and Incest*, Burns & Oates 1992.

Alison Webster

Selected Reading List

1 *Speaking from the Body*

Karen Armstrong, *The Gospel According to Woman*, Elmtree 1986

Rosemary Radford Ruether, *Sexism and God-Talk*, SCM Press 1992

Elaine Pagels, *The Gnostic Gospels*, Weidenfeld and Nicholson 1979

Julian of Norwich, *Revelations of Divine Love*, Image Books 1977

2 *Speaking from the Edge*

Elaine Graham and Margaret Halsey, *Life Cycles*, SPCK 1993

Toril Moi (ed.), *French Feminist Thought*, Blackwell 1987

Rosemary Radford Ruether, *Gaia and God*, SCM Press and HarperCollins 1993

Elizabeth Stuart, *Daring to Speak Love's Name: A Gay and Lesbian Prayer Book*, Hamish Hamilton 1993

Susan Brooks Thistlethwaite, *Sex, Race and God: Christian Feminism in Black and White*, Crossroad Publishing 1989

Rosemary Tong, *Feminist Thought: A Comprehensive Introduction*, Unwin Hyman 1989

3 *Speaking from the Text*

Elizabeth Cady Stanton, *The Woman's Bible*, Polygon 1985

Chung Hyun Kyung, *Struggle to be the Sun Again*, SCM Press and Orbis Books 1991

Patricia Demers, *Women as Interpreters of the Bible*, Paulist Press 1992

Letty Russell (ed.), *Feminist Interpretation of the Bible*, Blackwell and Westminster Press 1985

Elisabeth Schüssler Fiorenza, *Bread not Stone: The Challenge of Feminist Biblical Interpretation*, T&T Clark 1990

Phyllis Trible, *God and the Rhetoric of Sexuality*, SCM Press and Fortress Press 1992 and *Texts of Terror*, SCM Press and Fortress Press 1992

4 *Speaking for Ourselves*

Lavinia Byrne (ed.), *The Hidden Tradition: Women's Spiritual Writings Re-Discovered*, SPCK 1991

Joan Chittister, OSB, *Womanstrength: Modern Church, Modern Women*, Sheed and Ward, 1990

Daphne Hampson, *Theology and Feminism*, Blackwell 1990

Elisabeth Schüssler Fiorenza, *In Memory of Her: A Feminist Theological Reconstruction of Christian Origins*, SCM Press and Crossroad Publishing 1983

Ann Loades (ed.), *Feminist Theology: A Reader*, SPCK 1991

Carol Noren, *The Woman in the Pulpit*, Abingdon Press 1991

WCC, *WWC Decade in Solidarity with Women Resource Book*, WCC Publications 1988

5 *Speaking into the Silence*

Carol Christ, *Diving Deep and Surfacing: Women Writers on the Spiritual Quest*, Beacon Press 1980

Kathy Galloway, *Imagining the Gospels*, SPCK 1988

Saint Hilda Community, *Women Included*, SPCK 1991

Sara Maitland, *Daughters of Jerusalem*, Blond and Briggs 1978, reissued Virago 1993

Janet Morley, *All Desires Known*, Movement for the Ordination of Women and Women in Theology 1988; new edition SPCK 1992

Alicia Ostriker, 'Thieves of Language: Women Poets and Revisionist Mythmaking' in Elaine Showalter (ed.), *The New Feminist Criticism: Essays on Women, Literature and Theory*, Virago 1986

Alice Walker, *The Color Purple*, The Women's Press 1983

Contributors

Hazel Addy is the United Reformed Church's National AIDS Adviser.

Jan Berry is a member of the ecumencial chaplaincy team at Sheffield Hallam University and previously worked for twelve years as a team minister in Baptist/United Reformed churches in Manchester. She has a particular interest in developing women-centred liturgy and ritual and is a member of Women in Theology.

Sarah Brewerton is a minister of the United Reformed Church serving at Chorlton Central Baptist/United Reformed Church and at Withington Hospital in Manchester.

Lavinia Byrne IBVM is Associate Secretary for the Community of Women and Men for the Council of Churches for Britain and Ireland.

'Carol' is a theologian, pastor and teacher.

Kate Compston is a minister of the United Reformed Church.

Mary Cotes is minister at South Street Baptist Church, Exeter.

Susan Durber is minister of Salford Central United Reformed Church and a tutor at the Northern Baptist College.

Kathy Galloway is a Church of Scotland minister and a former co-warden of Iona Abbey. Her publications include *Imagining the Gospels* (SPCK 1988) and *Love Burning Deep* (SPCK 1993).

Margaret Hebblethwaite is Assistant Editor of *The Tablet*. Her publications include *Motherhood and God* (Chapman 1984) and *Six New Gospels: New Testament Women Tell Their Stories* (Chapman 1994).

Margaret Kennedy is a Roman Catholic and a survivor of child sexual abuse. She founded Christian Survivors of Sexual Abuse. She is committed to challenging the oppression of sexual violence against all children.

Janet Lees is an Honorary Consultant Speech and Language Therapist working with brain injured children at the Hospital for Sick Children, Great Ormond Street, London, and an Ordinand of the United Reformed Church, training at Mansfield College, Oxford and the University of Natal, Pietermaritzburg, South Africa.

Ann Loades is Reader in Theology at Durham University and has edited *Feminist Theology – A Reader* (SPCK 1990).

Pam Lunn is a member of the Religious Society of Friends (Quakers). She teaches at Woodbrooke, the Quaker adult education college in Selly Oak, Birmingham. Her interests are in post-Christian feminist spirituality and the issue of Whiteness in feminism.

Sara Maitland is a novelist and theologian. Her publications include *Daughters of Jerusalem* (Blond and Briggs 1978; Virago 1993) and *A Map of the New Country* (Routledge and Kegan Paul 1983).

Alison Peacock is a Research Associate with the European Contact Group on Urban Industrial Mission.

Janet Martin Soskice is a lecturer within the Faculty of Divinity at Cambridge University.

Janet Morley is Adult Education Adviser of Christian Aid. Her publications include *All Desires Known* (MOW/WIT 1988; new edition SPCK 1992) and *Bread for Tomorrow* (SPCK 1992).

Bridget Rees is Christian Aid Area Secretary for Gloucestershire, Hereford and Worcester.

Nicola Slee is Director of Studies at the Aston Training Scheme. She has published widely in the fields of religious education and feminist theology, as well as some poetry and liturgical material.

Helen Stanton is Anglican Chaplain to the University of Sheffield.

Elizabeth Stuart is Senior Lecturer in Theology at the College of St Mark and St John, Plymouth. Among her publications are *Through Brokenness* (Fount 1990) and *Daring to Speak Love's Name* (Hamish Hamilton 1992). She is a trustee of the Institute for the Study of Christianity and Sexuality.

Elizabeth Templeton is a freelance theologian and writer. She has edited *A Woman's Place: Women at Work* (St Andrews Press 1993).

Angela Tilby is a programme maker for the BBC.

Hazel Walton is a Methodist Lay Preacher and a Community Worker.

Heather Walton is a Methodist Lay Preacher and a tutor at the Northern Baptist College.

Alison Webster works for the Institute for the Study of Christianity and Sexuality.

Janet Wootton is minister of Union Chapel, Islington and a former President of the Congregational Federation.